O9-BUD-016

Praise for
Who Told You That You Were Naked?

"A book that grips the mind and warms the heart as it sweeps away a lot of the hang-ups we have about sin, guilt, punishment and how these fit with a loving God. John Jacob Raub says so many things we all need to hear."

—WILLIAM H. SHANNON

"His sources are impeccably classical; his interpretation startlingly radical; yet to this reader uncannily accurate. Profound . . ."

—DAVID BURRELL

"A healing balm. It deserves a wide readership."

—BROTHER PATRICK HART, O.C.S.O.

"Bright sunny days and soft spring rain fall on both an Al Capone and on Chicago's Little Sisters of the Poor. All people benefit from God's goodness. All are recipients of his love. . . . But we don't like the kingdom of God—until we accept that we *are included in those* all whom *God is loving all the time. When we accept that we too our being showered with mercy upon mercy, then we can allow others to be so showered. We can allow the kingdom of God to come, or rather, we can accept that* it is already here."*

—From *Who Told You That You Were Naked?*

Who Told You
That You Were Naked?

To Carol
with prayers
Fr Jual
Gethsemani

Feb 1994

Who Told You
That You Were Naked?

*Freedom from Judgment, Guilt
and Fear of Punishment*

John Jacob Raub

CROSSROAD · NEW YORK

1995

The Crossroad Publishing Company
370 Lexington Avenue, New York, NY 10017

Copyright © 1992 by John Jacob Raub

All rights reserved. No part of this book may be reproduced,
stored in a retrieval system, or transmitted, in any form or by any means,
electronic, mechanical, photocopying, recording, or otherwise, without
the written permission of The Crossroad Publishing Company.

Printed in the United States of America

Library of Congress Cataloging-in-Publication Data

Raub, John Jacob.
   Who told you that you were naked? : freedom from judgment, guilt
and fear of punishment / John Jacob Raub.
      p.   cm.
   ISBN 0-8245-1203-0 (pbk.)
   1. Peace of mind—Religious aspects—Christianity.   2. Guilt—
Religious aspects—Christianity.   3. Fear of God.   4. Punishment—
Religious aspects—Christianity.   5. Judgment of God.   6. God—Love.
I. Title.
BV4908.5.R38 1992
233' .4—dc20   92-12830
                                                          CIP

*In gratitude to those who taught me
not to be ashamed of my nakedness*

Acknowledgments

I acknowledge my indebtedness to Fr. Carl Kish, a priest of the Diocese of Youngstown, Ohio. A little over two years ago, Carl first introduced me to many of the ideas expressed in the following pages.

In his subsequent visits to the monastery he further shared his insights. This work is the result of those insights coupled with similar ideas suggested to me by books and articles. Chief among these is the book *A Course in Miracles.*

I am also grateful to my abbot, Fr. Timothy Kelly, and to Fr. Hilarion Schmock, a monk of Gethsemani. Both have listened with patience and understanding as I endeavored to clarify my thoughts.

There are others, including Sr. Marguerite Holz, H.M., who have helped by their suggestions. These know who they are and of my gratitude to them.

Finally, my sincere thanks is due to my cousin, Mrs. William (Marianna) Neal, who spent many hours typing and proofreading the original manuscript, and to Jack Wheeler, who provided ideas and the incentive to seek publication. If it were not for Marianna and Jack, this book would never have been born.

Contents

Introduction

Original sin is depicted in Genesis as the tempter telling humanity to eat the fruit and "you will be like gods who know what is good and what is bad" (Gn 3:5).[1]

We fall for this temptation; we want to be "like the gods." "The gods" are our goal and we want to be imitators of these idols.

We envision these idols as perfect, right, strong and powerful. They symbolize success, however each of us imagines success, and as such they are our ego ideals. Once we accept these ideals as something we must live up to, constant self-judgment and self-criticism are inevitable.

"The gods" provide our standard for "knowing what is good and what is bad." We continually judge ourselves accordingly: Am I "good" — perfect, right, strong and powerful, etc., or am I "bad" — imperfect, wrong, weak, etc. Am I measuring up and therefore successful, or am I not measuring up and therefore unsuccessful....

The compulsion to judge or to know "what is good and what is bad" is all-pervasive. We continually judge whether or not we are like we "should be," that is, "like the gods." And since we can never live up to graven images, we are doomed to judge *against* ourselves, *against* who we really are. In comparison to who we think we should be (our false selves), who we are (our true selves) will be seen as inferior. When we place who we are — human beings — against who we think we "should

---

[1]Unless otherwise indicated, Scripture references are from the New American Bible. The abbreviations JB and RSV refer to the Jerusalem Bible and the Revised Standard Version respectively.

be," the result is always self-condemnation. When we compare ourselves to a false ideal, the verdict will always be — "Guilty!"

The result, then, of humanity's eating of the tree of knowledge of good and bad is twofold:

First, the human mind is a judgmental one. We are constantly judging good and bad, which means we are continually dividing, separating, cutting off.

Second, since the primary object of our judging is ourselves, we become alien to our true selves. We judge ourselves to be guilty simply for being who we are, human beings, and so are interiorly divided.

Continual judging and its corollary, a guilt-induced inner alienation or split, is our experience of original sin.

·   ·   ·   ·

Self-alienation results in a feeling that we are separated not only from ourselves but also from God. We feel guilty because of a gap that we imagine exists between ourselves and the source of our being. We feel guilty for a fictional space. And once we judge ourselves as "guilty," fear follows. Fear always accompanies a sense of guilt; the two are inseparable. Fear is the most fundamental human emotion. The Genesis story continues, saying that after the fall God called to the human, "Where are you?" The human answered, "I heard you in the garden, but I was afraid…" (Gn 3:10). "I was afraid." Fear! Why? "…for I am naked." What was Adam saying? Why did being naked make him afraid?

Adam, or humanity, was saying, in effect, "In my naked humanity, my naked creatureliness, I am not like (i.e., I am separated from) the gods. I am therefore weak, bad, imperfect, wrong, unsuccessful. I am not what I should be. Because I feel guilty I am afraid and have hidden myself."

Then God asked Adam: "Who told you that you were naked?" (Gn 3:11). That is, "Who *told* you that you were bad? Who *told* you that you were not what you should be? …Humanity, who *told* you that you were separated from me, that you were guilty?" In asking Adam, "Who told you that you were naked," God was asking a fundamental question, one that we will discuss in the following pages. We will discuss judging, guilt and fear of punishment and how this leads to self-punishment which is the essence of sins.

Judgment, guilt and punishment, being common to everyone's experience, have been the concern of humankind from the beginning. These subjects, like the problem of evil to which they are closely associated, are a major theme in literature and drama as well as the various religious traditions throughout the ages.

A prime example of our struggle with guilt and consequently self-punishment is found in Greek mythology. And one of the best-known mythical characters is Prometheus. The monk Thomas Merton, a popular religious writer of this century, wrote a meditation on Prometheus.

Let us look at Merton's "Prometheus" as a preparation for our text. This prologue will serve as an introduction to many of the themes we will discuss in more detail.

Prologue

Prometheus

In ancient Greek mythology, Prometheus stole fire from the gods and as punishment Zeus had him chained to a rock, setting an eagle upon him to devour his liver. To make matters worse, the liver was constantly replenished, making Prometheus' punishment eternal.

Thomas Merton's meditation on Prometheus[1] describes this tragic Greek figure as "Guilty, frustrated, rebellious, fear ridden" (p. 17). "Guilt was the precious gift of the false gods to Prometheus, a gift that made all this waste possible" (p. 18). Merton understands the terrible punishment inflicted on Prometheus as his own desire to punish himself.

> He was strong enough [i.e., he had the power to] consume himself for all eternity in punishment for having desired their [the gods'] fire. In fact, he destroyed himself forever that they might live. For this reason, idolatry was, and is, the fundamental sin. (p. 20)

Prometheus gave birth to his gods, as we all do, thereby becoming his own judge and executioner. His illusions of guilt enabled him to blame Zeus for his punishment, when really it was Prometheus who sat in judgment and passed sentence on himself.

---

[1]Thomas Merton, "Prometheus: A Meditation," *The Behavior of Titans* (Norfolk, Conn.: New Directions, 1961), pp. 15–23.

Prometheus cannot conceive of a true victory, his own tri-
umph is to let the vulture devour his liver: he will be a martyr
and a victim, because the gods he has created in his own image
represent his own tyrannical demands upon himself. (p. 18)

He becomes his own vulture and is satisfied at last. (p. 17)

Paradoxically, it is Prometheus' own sense of guilt that gives the
gods their existence. The result is a dependent relationship where
Prometheus needs Zeus and Zeus needs Prometheus. Each depends on the
other in order to exist. "The guilt Prometheus felt from the beginning
was more necessary for his gods than for himself. If he had not been
guilty, such gods would not have been able to exist. Without guilt he
could not have conceived them, and since they only existed in his own
mind he had to be guilty in order to think of them at all" (p. 20). "By
his guilt he bore witness to his little household gods, his fire hoarders"
(p. 21). "In the eyes of Prometheus, to be himself was to be guilty, the
exercise of liberty was a crime, an attack upon the gods which he had
made" (p. 16).

Prometheus was caught in a double misconception, a two-fold illusion. First, he believed that his idols actually had power: "he confessed
that he...believed in their falsity" (p. 21). He "opened his heart to his
unreal gods" (p. 21). Second, he believed that he must steal from the
gods to get what he needed to live. He felt (correctly) that Zeus would
never give his power to humans. There was therefore only one course
open to him. In order to survive, he had to steal Zeus' fire, for "he knew
no god that would be willing to give it for nothing" (p. 19).

To shed our Promethean mind we must believe in the true God.
Through the eyes of faith we must be able to see that the "fire" of the
true God is not power but *freedom.* This insight into the nature of God
is the most significant difference between the idolater and the believer.
The idolater sees the gods in terms of power: Zeus' fire *is* power! The

believer sees G   terms of freedom: God's fire *is* freedom![2] Accordingly, the idolater thinks he must steal what he needs; the believer knows that freedom cannot be stolen. The believer realizes that the fire is not to be stolen but received as a gift. "There is nothing we can steal from God at all because before we can think of stealing it, it has already been given" (p. 23). "God cannot seek to keep anything good to Himself alone" (p. 22).

Not knowing about Christ and the freedom of God, "Prometheus thought he had to ascend into heaven to steal what God had already desired to give him" (p. 21). Prometheus did not know that "Christ came down with the fire [freedom] he needed" (p. 21), and "poured out upon us the fire of the Holy Spirit" (p. 22). Although Prometheus was unaware of it, "the fire he thought he had to steal from the gods is his own identity...his own spiritual freedom" (p. 16). Prometheus thought he needed power that resided outside of himself. What he really needed was his freedom that was already within him. We are all in search of freedom, of Christ residing within us — Christ, our true self.

Is it too frightening for us to shed our Promethean self for our Christ self? Can we renounce power, that capacity to judge ourselves, and so be unchained from our rock of self-punishment? Can we be what God wants us to be? Can we give ourselves permission to be who we are — children of God?

It is no small task to refuse to grab for the power of the gods and instead accept the terrifying freedom of the children of God, "the terror of having to be [ourselves]," which is "the affirmation and vindication of [our] own being as a sanctified creature in the image of God" (p. 16).

It is terrifying to accept our own identity in God, our spiritual freedom, for that requires us to change our mind about who God is, about who we are and about who Christ is. God is not Zeus; we are not

---

[2]When we see Christian prayers referring to our God as the "God of power and might," one wonders who is praying to which god? Some prayers sound more like a chained Prometheus praying to Zeus than a free son or daughter praying to their "Abba."

Prometheus; Christ is not Prometheus. We tend not only to mis-identify ourselves, we mis-identify God and his Christ.

Often we see Christ not as a sign of God's freedom and love but rather as another Prometheus who through much suffering obtained the power of the gods to make everything and everyone the way they "should be," that is, the way *we* think that they "should be."

Merton comments on what happened when Christians thought of Christ as another Prometheus:

> They justified wars and crusades and pogroms and the bomb and Auschwitz. Michelangelo's Christ of the Last Judgment in the Sistine Chapel is precisely this Promethean Christ... whipping sinners with his great Greek muscles.[3]

By making Christ a judge and then taking that fictional judge as our model, Merton says, we blow up the wedding feast of the Gospel, that feast which is supposed to include everyone, and "that is the way men judge themselves" (p. 16). We become "Christlike," actually, "Promethean-like," and judge all those God has invited to the wedding feast, starting with ourselves. We judge ourselves as guilty and then look around for someone on whom we can throw our self-punishment. And if at the moment no one is handy for us to blow up (there usually is, however), we can always, Promethean-like, gnaw at our innards for eternity.

Who is God, a jealous father holding on to his power? "The small gods we have made for ourselves are jealous fathers" (p. 15). Or is God the father of our freedom? How we answer that question determines how we regard ourselves. If we see God as one of the gods (one of those "jealous fathers"), we will see ourselves as the guilty thief, Prometheus, and so we will see ourselves as being forever chained to our rock of masochistic punishment. "The person who does not know the living God is condemned by his gods to this despair" (p. 15).

---

[3]As quoted in an article by Msgr. William Shannon, "Thomas Merton and Judaism," *America,* October 6, 1990, p. 220.

On the other hand, if we know the living God of freedom, we know that he has given us everything; he wills that we have the fire. He wills his freedom to be ours. "The fire [freedom] was something God did not need for Himself since he made it especially for us" (p. 19). "The fire [is ours] for the asking, a gift of the true God" (p. 18), and "that fire attracts [us] more than [we] believe possible, because it is in reality [our] own" (p. 17).

In commenting on his meditation, Merton explains why the fire of God, that is, God's freedom, his love, his life — everything — is really ours.

> Everything is mine precisely because everything is God's. If it were not God's, it could never be mine. If it could not be mine, God would not even want it for Himself. And all that is God's is His very Self. All that God gives me becomes, in some way, my own self. What then is mine? God is mine. And what is God's? I am God's. But when this becomes clear, there is no place left in the picture for anything resembling Prometheus.[4]

Indeed, "one who loves Christ is not allowed to be Prometheus" (p. 18). For "realizing [our] divine sonship in Christ and in the Spirit of fire who has been given us" (p. 16), we know we "must keep this fire that is given [us] and [we] must assert that fire is [ours]" (p. 18). God has decreed the fire is ours by right, to be received gratefully, but never stolen, never struggled for. "To struggle with the gods seems great indeed to those who do not know…that God is on our side…and defeat is not permissible" (p. 18). And once we know that the fire has been given us by the true God, "[we] must maintain [our] rights against all the false gods who hold that it was stolen" (p. 18).

"We must maintain our rights against the false gods." In the face of their insistence on punishment we must maintain our innocence. We

---

[4]Thomas Merton, *The New Man* (New York: Farrar, Straus and Cudahy, 1961), p. 37.

must refuse to judge ourselves as guilty just because we are human beings — and naked humans at that!

Unlike Prometheus, we did not steal from God. Rather, we were given everything as a gift. Right in our nakedness we were given our identity as the Children of God, our Christlikeness. And we were given this Divine Freedom by our "Abba," who loves us the way we were created — naked!

Unfortunately, we refuse to believe in this unconditional love and so we reject our identity as God's children. Living out the Prometheus-Zeus conflict we reject the freedom of God and his kingdom — God's world! We then try to create our own identity, our own world, a world based on the illusion of separation.

Part One

Our World

I have chosen you out of the world.
Jn 15:19

Be not conformed to this world.
Rm 12:2

Our world, the world we see, is a reflection of our self-image. We picture the world in the image we hold of ourselves. We see what *we judge we are*. We judge only our mirror. Our world is a world of judging; since judgment involves guilt, our world is a world of guilt.

We carry within us a massive amount of guilt, not only a behavioral guilt, but a more basic existential guilt — guilt not for our actions, but for our being. It is this primordial sense of guilt, not for what we have done, but for *who* we are, that colors all our relationships, shades everything we see.

Theologically, this fundamental guilt, this guilt we feel from the mere fact that we are human beings, is associated with original sin. This sense of guilt is based on the illusion of separation and alienation. And this illusion, namely that we are split off from God, is the basis for our dualistic thinking. It is the "bad dream" all humans dream. We mistakenly feel we are split off from God, others and even ourselves, and we are therefore not what we "should be"; we feel we are bad, wrong, inferior, guilty. To be more exact, this guilt could be called shame. It's our original shame.

Psychologically this phenomenon has been described in various ways. Alfred Adler saw all human beings as laboring under a burden of inferiority. Sigmund Freud saw human beings as burdened by the

21

misunderstood or frightening sexual drives and experiences of childhood. But what is common to these explanations, be they theological or psychological, is an underlying sense of guilt and its accompanying fear of punishment.

•   •   •   •

We feel ashamed that we are not what we "should be," for we are *just* human beings. Our very humanness becomes a source of our guilt. We have opted to be like we "should be," that is, "like the gods," our idols ("eat the fruit and be like the gods").

Since our humanness falls short of our impossible goal (idols are never real), guilt and fear are our constant companions. It is through the lenses of this guilt and fear that we create the world we see. The outer world becomes merely a projection of our inner world. The world we see becomes nothing more than the reflection of the judgment we are placing on ourselves — "Guilty! Punishment due!"

We project onto others our interior split by which one part of us is judging the other part. People and situations become for us merely windows through which we see our inner division and alienation. Then we deceive ourselves into believing that our problems are *outside* of us.

But the conflicts we see as arising in other people and situations are a reflection of our self-condemnation, externalized onto other people and situations. The picture we take of others is the view we have of ourselves. When we see others are not what they "should be," it merely reflects what we feel — that we are not what we "should be."

So we see the world in terms of our dualistic, judgmental mind. Indeed, it is impossible for us to see the world in any way other than the way we see ourselves. The external world is our internal world. Since we are internally divided and separated we naturally see a divided and separated world. Since we place ourselves under judgment, we naturally place the world under judgment. If we see guilt and punishment as our due, we will automatically see the world as guilty and deserving of punishment. The world we see is definitely our world, for in it we behold ourselves.[1]

• • • •

Our world is the one we view from the perspective of our personal dividedness. We have invented an external world of conflict from our inner world of conflict. What we "should be" conflicts with what we are. Our internal dualism forms our model for judgment. Upon these scales we continually weigh what is right and good against what is wrong and bad. We carry around within us a paradigm of justice which we super-impose on everyone and everything. We have a definite game plan that encases all of reality, a certain set of rules that we lay on life.

Accordingly, we are continually judging others and situations: good/bad, right/wrong, innocent/guilty, should be/should not be, reward-able/punishable. This is the world we have created, a world of division and separation. We understand this world and feel at home in it. It makes sense to us.

Depending on our sphere of influence and our degree of power, we can manage and control our world to some degree. It may be stressful, even difficult at times, but it is at least understandable; it may be de-manding, but it is workable. Workable, understandable, controllable, manageable — that's our world. That's the world that makes us feel se-cure. That's why we created it. That's the world we have made, the one we think "should be." It's a dualistic world of judgment and "should's," filled with guilt, fear and punishment, but it is the world we have chosen for the security it offers us.

---

[1] In a symbolic way Christ told us that we behold ourselves in what we see: "the lamp of the body is the eye" (Mt 6:22); "take care then that the light *in* you not become darkness" (Lk 11:35); "for if the light *in* you is darkness, how great will be the darkness [everywhere]" (Mt 6:23).

Security and Fear

We created our world from what others told us, either through their words or actions; others who at one time provided our security. We are tied to our judgmental world with its guilt and punishment because we are tied to the people who formed us.

The basis for our judgments is founded on what we learned from these key people in our lives. These people make up "our gods." Parental gods, church gods, state gods, teacher gods, peer gods, friend gods. Eat the fruit and be "like gods" (Gn 3:5).

From these idols we developed our model of good and bad, of what "should be" and what "should not be." From them we developed our game plan, our set of rules which is the basis for all our judgments. These gods are now internalized; we carry them around in our head and look to them for support. Self-judging, with its guilt, fear and punishment, holds us and our world together. It ties us to our idols and keeps our relationship with the gods intact.

By judging ourselves we are obeying the gods. We are doing what they told us to do. We are knowing (judging) "the good and the bad." Judging is the very "stuff" of our security; it is the glue that bonds us to our guardians within. And no matter how painful or how destructive that bond may be, we don't want to undo it.

• • • •

Closely connected with our need for security is *fear*. Fear arises whenever we feel we will be punished and/or abandoned by those whom we see as our protectors, our inner custodians. We are deathly afraid that in punishment for not being like we "should be," the bond with our idols will be broken and we will be abandoned, left to ourselves to face the harshness of life.

In the story of original sin, we see the connection between guilt, fear and sins in the sense that guilt and fear lead to our sins.[2] Adam (literally, "the one from the earth"), in answer to God's question as to why he had hidden himself, said simply, "I was afraid" (Gn 3:10). Seeing himself as guilty and mistakenly thinking God would see him the same way, Adam became afraid and passed judgment on himself.

Adam (humanity) was afraid God would punish him for his "sin," so he hid himself. In other words, he moved against himself, he acted contrary to who he was. This destructive counter-motion is the root of sins. Each one of our sins is a going against our true selves. Moreover, our sins are begotten by feelings of guilt and fear.[3]

• • • •

Since there is a causal link between fear and sins, it follows that salvation, which is the removal of sins, must include the removal of fear. Accordingly, the Scriptures repeatedly describe salvation in terms of eradicating fear.

Salvation history began with the Old Covenant made with Abraham and God's words "fear not Abram" (Gn 15:1). When the New Covenant began, again the first words were "fear not": "Fear not, Mary" (Lk 1:30). Both the Old and New Covenants therefore began with "Fear not." When it came time for the birth of our Savior, an angel announced to the shepherds of Bethlehem, "Do not be afraid, for behold I proclaim to you good news of great joy" (Lk 2:10). And it was this "good news," or this

---

[2] In a later chapter we will discuss the difference between "sin" — the illusion that we are separated from God and therefore not what we should be — and "sins" — our self-destructive thoughts, words and deeds.

[3] When we find ourselves caught in sinful habits, it may be helpful to ask ourselves: "Of what am I afraid?" If we push that question far enough, I think we will find endless possibilities, but ultimately we are afraid of death.

gospel (since the words are synonymous), that Christ continually proclaimed during his public ministry.

In the four gospels there are approximately a dozen references where Jesus tells his hearers to "fear not." Of even greater significance is the frequency of "Do not be afraid," which is found in the post-resurrection appearances.[4] "Do not fear" or its positive equivalent "Peace be with you"[5] is the expression used to announce Christ's resurrection and the completion of our salvation. From even a cursory reading of the gospels, we learn that our salvation involves the elimination of fear. This is certainly good news!

• • • •

It must be admitted, however, that there are certain verses of the Bible that speak of fear as good and even something to be desired. In the psalms we read: "The fear of the Lord is Holy" (Ps 19:10); "I shall teach you the fear of the Lord" (Ps 34:12); "The fear of the Lord is the beginning of wisdom" (Ps 111:10). But the fear that is spoken of in these psalms is not a servile fear; it is not the fear of punishment.

Rather this "fear of the Lord" is a profound reverence before God. It is respect tinged with awe, in beholding the goodness and love of God. Servile fear cannot exist with love, nor fear of punishment with friendship. Thus, shortly before the end of his earthly life, Christ told his followers: "I no longer call you servants...but friends" (Jn 15:15). Christ sought to elicit love from his hearers, not fear; he wanted friends, not servants.

• • • •

There is, nevertheless, one place in the gospels where it *appears* that Jesus is telling his hearers to fear God, or at least to fear the punishment of God. The gospel of Matthew (10:28) quotes Jesus as saying, "Do not

---

[4]See Mt 28:5; 10.
[5]See Jn 20:19, 21, 26.

be afraid of those who kill the body but cannot kill the soul; rather be afraid of the one who can destroy both body and soul in Gehenna."[6]

This statement raises the question as to whether or not God actually punishes us. In a later chapter we will discuss that question more thoroughly. May it suffice here to say that God is not mentioned at all in this verse. Jesus says only, "...be afraid of *the one* who can destroy both body and soul in Gehenna [hell]."

Most of us automatically *assume* that God is *"The One* who can destroy..." This assumption says more about our mind-set than it does about God's revelation — for in the gospels, God is always depicted as the giver of life, not its destroyer. Besides, nowhere in any of the four gospels does Jesus tell us that we should fear God. On the contrary, rather than tell us we should fear God, Jesus boldly insisted that we call God "Abba." Although we translate "Abba" as "Father," it is, in fact, a nickname of tender affection more like our word "Daddy."

Of all the world's prophets and religious leaders, no one other than Jesus ever dared say that we should address God with such filial buoyancy and trust as "Abba" implies. To assume, then, that Jesus is identifying God, our "daddy," as "the one who can destroy both body and soul in hell" goes contrary to the whole tenor of his thought. This is especially true of what immediately follows those words.

There Jesus continues: "Are not two sparrows sold for a small coin? Yet not one of them falls without your Father's knowledge. Even all the hairs of your head are counted. So do not be afraid; you are worth more than many sparrows" (Mt 10:29–31). The preceding verses (Mt 10:28) must be read in this context. To overlook this point by identifying God as our destroyer does violence to the very sense of the entire passage which is one of confidence in God's love along with fearless reliance on

---

[6]Gehenna, a valley southwest of Jerusalem, was once a center of an idolatrous cult in which children were offered in fiery sacrifice to "the gods." Often our word "hell" is used instead of "Gehenna." I think it worthy of note that, when Christ wanted to describe the ultimate in human destructiveness, he chose this place associated with idolatry. See note for 5:22 in the New American Bible.

Divine providence. Abba is a life-giver, never a destroyer — one to be trusted, not feared.

•   •   •   •

We may question: "Whom shall we fear if not God?" Who is "the one"? Ourselves! We are to be watchful about ourselves! It is our own self-destructiveness that we must "fear," i.e., be on the alert about. For it is we alone who can destroy ourselves both physically and spiritually. We are to be on guard against deadly tendencies fermenting within us by which we truly can "destroy both body and soul in hell."

It is with this understanding of "fear" that we are to read these Matthean verses and also St. Paul's exhortation to the Philippians. "Work out your salvation with fear and trembling" (Ph 2:12). Again this does *not* mean we should be afraid of God. To so interpret "fear and trembling" would be to go contrary to the theme of this letter which has been called "the letter of joy." "Rejoice in the Lord, again I say rejoice" (Ph 4:4). "I rejoice greatly in the Lord" (Ph 4:10). Rather, "fear and trembling" is an Old Testament expression indicating "awe and serious-ness in the service of God."[7]

St. Paul is telling his new converts at Philippi that just as the true believers of the old dispensation lived their Mosaic law with watchful earnestness, so too the followers of Jesus are to take seriously their Christian vocation and pay diligent attention to the matter of their salva-tion. A Christian's joyful trust in God is meant to foster internal freedom, not be a cause for external laxity, and we have to be vigilant about that. We are therefore to work out our salvation with "fear and trembling."

•   •   •   •

Scripture's final word as to whether or not fear of punishment should be part of a Christian's attitude is found in the first letter of St.

---

[7]See note for Ph 2:12 in the New American Bible.

John, one of the latest works of the New Testament. In this letter, we find the most fully developed and mature understanding of Christian love vis-à-vis servile fear. "Love will come to its perfection in us when we can face the day of judgment *without fear*... In love there can be *no fear*, but fear is driven out by perfect love ['Perfect love casts out fear' (RSV)] because to fear is to expect punishment and anyone who *is afraid* is still imperfect in love" (I Jn 4:17–18; emphasis added).

In the same letter is stated the reason there is to be no fear in a Christian's love for God. Immediately prior to the above we read, "We ourselves have known and put our faith in God's love toward ourselves. God *is* love and anyone who lives in love, lives in God and God in him" (I Jn 4:16 JB). To fear God would be a denial of God's love for us which, in effect, would be a denial of God, as "God is love." When we fear God we turn the true God into an idol; we turn our loving Abba into one of "the gods" whose function we feel is to judge and punish us.

And can there be any greater blasphemy? Is not to fear God and to separate ourselves from God's love the one "unforgivable sin" of which our Lord spoke? "Whoever blasphemes against the Holy Spirit [God's Love] will never have forgiveness but is guilty of an everlasting sin" (Mk 3:29). Our fear has made any forgiveness impossible because we don't believe in God's loving forgiveness. We don't believe *God is love!*

Conversely, and happily for us, to be free from fear is to be freed from the tyrannical lords of our own making. But as we have seen, there is a part of us that does not want to be freed from our idols and their "power." For the sake of our sense of security, we would rather live in guilt and fear before our "gods" than live in the freedom of God's love.

Because of our craving for safety, the path which leads from fear to freedom is difficult. So much so that in Christian spirituality the pathway to freedom is often referred to as *the way of the cross.*

The Cross

The cross frees us from our split judgmental world with its guilt, fear and self-punishment. The cross frees us from our inner alienation where the false self (who we think we "should be") punishes our true self (who we really are). The cross involves a refusal to move against ourselves, a refusal to punish or attack ourselves, a refusal to hold onto guilt and fear, and a refusal to stay in the hell of self-judgment.

The cross is the great paradox. It appears to symbolize pain, but actually the cross symbolizes the *shedding* of pain. Paradoxically, however, that shedding of pain is painful; letting go of suffering itself involves suffering.

How can the shedding of pain be painful? How can the refusal to hold onto suffering involve suffering? How can *not* hurting ourselves hurt so much? It is the same way that the shedding of the painful limitations of childhood (its dependence, anxieties, fears) and growing into the freedom of adulthood is painful. It is the pain associated with new life.

Both spiritual and physical adulthood involves a letting go of our sense of security. The world of the immature, whether spiritual or natural, *is* a world of suffering, but it does provide safety. The world of the immature is held together by guilt and pain but it also offers us shelter. This is the protection we feel when we are in our dualistic world. This is the "at homeness" we experience when we judge good/bad, right/wrong, and condemn or reward accordingly.

Letting go of that judging and condemning is the painful experience we call the cross because it demands that we leave our feelings of "at homeness." Not to judge and condemn shatters our secure world. Since

30

we created our world in the image of our idols, to let go of that world is going to make us feel very insecure; it is going to make us feel very disobedient. To leave our world we will have to disobey all those "should be's" which we learned from our idols. For only by disregarding our "should be's" will we be free enough to accept reality, to accept God's world, the kingdom of God, in whatever is.

In practice, accepting whatever is or its equivalent, living in the kingdom of God, is as "simple" as saying "that's all right." It is as simple and as difficult, for it is difficult to recognize life's injustices and inequalities, its pains and losses, and still maintain that life is all right, that God is present in all reality. To hold onto that conviction is crucifying because it demands the death of our false self, that comfortable home of "the gods."

To leave the shelter provided by our idols is painful, with the pain implied in our Lord's words: "If anyone comes to me without turning his back on his father and mother...indeed his very self [false self], he cannot be my follower" (Lk 14:26). But it is the pain of freedom not slavery, the pain of healing not punishment, the pain of growth not stagnation. It is birthing pain, not death pain.

By the cross we accept our true identity (true self). We become who we are, the innocent children of the Father, rather than who we are not, the guilty children of idols. The children of idols are always guilty, always fearful, always in punishment because they are always under judgment. As Christ once told his hearers: "The Devil is your father..." (Jn 8:44 JB), that is, "You are under judgment — your own!" To be forever condemning ourselves is to have the devil for our father, to be a child of idols.

On the other hand, the child of the true Father is always innocent, always guiltless and always at peace because the child of God, or "Son of God," is free of judgment. "There is no condemnation [judgment] for those who are in Christ Jesus" (i.e., those living their true selves) (Rom 8:1). Salvation involves nothing more and nothing less than changing our minds about who our father is.

Who *is* our Father? Do we keep our idols as our father and be condemned, or do we take God as our Father and be accepted? Do we choose
to be slaves or to be free? Do we hold onto our judgmental mind or are
we willing to have the mind of Christ — that mind which refuses to
condemn itself? To have this "mind of Christ," or to use another Pauline
expression, to be "in Christ," means to accept our oneness with God,
our innocence, to accept that *in Christ* we have no guilt, to accept that
we are the free children of God; that acceptance is the cross in our lives.

But why is it so crucifying to accept the fact that we have no guilt,
no shame, for being who we are — human beings? What is so crucifying about seeing ourselves as innocent? Don't we want to see
ourselves as innocent? *No!* But to see ourselves as innocent sounds as if
it would be easy. *It's not!* It is excruciatingly difficult because to see our
true selves as innocent breaks our ties with our idols. The bond that we
have established with our security figures is based on guilt; to deny
guilt, then, is to break that bond. We need to hold onto our feelings of
guilt because we are guilty in relation to our idols; take away our guilt
and that relationship collapses; take away our guilt and we lose our
supports.

Original innocence is much more difficult to accept than original
guilt, so much so that outside of Christ only his mother accepted her innocence completely: "all ages to come shall call me blessed" (Lk 1:48).
It *is* crucifying to be who we are, the innocent children of God, rather
than who we are not, the guilty offspring of idols. It *is* crucifying to be
who we are. For we are "just" human beings, whereas we want to
be "like the gods." We want to be like our idols, like we "should be."
It *is* crucifying to be who we are, for it demands we let go of who we
are not.

Changing our mind about who we are and what our world is necessarily follows changing our mind about who our father is. The two are
inseparable; really they are one and the same. That change of mind about
who our father is and then who we are is the cross; it is painful yet joyful, frightening yet freeing.

The cross is the most recognized symbol of Christianity, but unfortunately the most misunderstood. We tend to see it in negative rather than in positive terms, as something that diminishes rather than enlarges us. We see the cross as a sign of our guilt rather than the ultimate sign of our innocence, of condemnation, rather than liberation, of separation from, rather than union with God. If we could see with the eyes of faith we would see the cross as a sign of perfect freedom, and so be able to pray before our crucified God:

Thank you, God, for becoming a human being —
  so I don't have to be like the gods.
Thank you for becoming finite, limited —
  so I don't have to be infinite, unlimited.
Thank you for becoming mortal —
  so I don't have to try to be immortal.
Thank you for becoming inferior —
  so I and others don't have to be superior.
For being weak —
  so I and others don't have to be strong.
For being imperfect —
  so I and others don't have to be perfect.
For being disapproved —
  so I and others don't have to be approved.
God, thank you for being wrong —
  so I and others don't have to be right.
For being a failure —
  so I and others don't have to be a success.
For being poor in every way —
  so I and others don't have to be rich in any way.

Christ on the Cross, thank you for being different from my idols, so I don't have to hate myself and others for being different from those images I have created to support and hold me up.

Thank you for becoming all the things I think I should not be, so I don't have to kill myself and others trying to be all the things I think I should be.

Crucified God, thank you for becoming everything I despise about myself, so I can love myself and others in you.

I can love you — who by your humanity have joined yourself with me right at that point where I most dislike myself.

God — thank you for being crucified, so I can be free.

Freedom

Nothing ever has been more insupportable for a man and
human society than freedom...which men fear and dread.[8]

The only obstacle to our freedom is our fear of being free. Our freedom
is frightening! It is frightening to be cut off from our props, to be loos-
ened from our inner supports. It is a terrifying experience to let go of our
"gods," to forsake our idols. And if we have created God in the image of
our "gods" we will be tied to God just as we have been tied to our other
"gods," through guilt and punishment.

If we turn God into just one more, albeit the greatest of our security
figures, we will relate to him not as free children to our Abba, but as
guilty illegitimate offspring deserving of punishment. As harsh as that
last alternative sounds, that is the one we are tempted to choose. We are
tempted to deny our true identity as God's free children and instead
choose guilt over innocence, punishment over pardon, slavery over freedom, and these destructive choices can be made in an almost infinite
number of ways — conscious or unconscious — both equally deadly.

We are tempted to choose punishment over freedom, which is a
choice for death over life, for several related reasons, the first being control. We can manage a relationship built on guilt and punishment better
than one built on freedom. We don't want our freedom because we cannot control a free relationship with God but we *can* control a relationship
built on guilt. We cannot control our salvation if it is a free gift of God,
but we *can* control it if it is based on judgment and punishment. We can

---

[8]Fyodor Dostoevsky, *The Brothers Karamazof,* Great Books of the Western
World, vol. 52 (Chicago: William Benton Publisher, 1952), p. 130.

judge ourselves as guilty, punish or move against ourselves, and then be assured of God's favor. Through our self-imposed suffering we can weigh the scales so that God owes us something — namely salvation! By refusing freedom and instead holding onto guilt and self-punishment, we control our destiny to the degree that we become our own savior. By hurting ourselves, we save ourselves. Or so we think.

Another reason we so readily move against (punish) ourselves rather than accept the freedom to be who we truly are is that punishment is the means we use to identify with "the gods." Because we see God not as the source of our freedom but as one of "the gods" who punishes us, we in turn punish ourselves. Our basic temptation is to "be like the gods" and "the gods" are those whom we fear will punish us for falling short of our goal, for not being like we should be; so we imitate their punitive role and punish ourselves. Fear of punishment leads to self-punishment! What we fear, that "the gods" would accuse and punish us, we do to ourselves. We see this phenomenon in children who assume the punitive role of their parents and punish themselves. By punishing themselves these children can identify with their parents and so *become* the parents even at the expense of hurting themselves.

Fear of punishment leading to self-punishment is an application of the maxim "If you can't beat 'em, join 'em," that is, "do what they do." And the reason we want to "do what 'the gods' do" is that we want to identify with them, we want to become them, we want their power, their life. By punishing ourselves we are grabbing for what we imagine to be Divine Power, which we equate with the very life of "the gods."

There are benefits attached to our self-punishment, our self-inflicted pain. We have a stake in holding onto our suffering; it pays a dividend and that dividend is power. Alfred Adler saw humans as developing the will to power to compensate for feelings of inferiority. Freud, in his theory of the Oedipal complex, saw the child as striving to seize the power of the father. These psychological explanations fit well into the theology of Genesis. Eat the fruit "and you will be like gods..." (Gn 3:5). Our drive to be like "the gods" is basically a drive to obtain their power, to assume their role, to have their life. By having the power

to punish ourselves we become "the gods" of our imagination, we become our idols, but the cost is denying who we are. The cost is our own destruction.

By moving against ourselves, by punishing and attacking ourselves, we set up a masochistic relationship with "the gods" where we become *both* the victim *and* the victor. We lose our freedom but we gain the "power of the gods." We win by losing.

The irony of our throwing away our freedom for the sake of the power or life of "the gods" is that "the gods" don't have life. "The gods" are idols; they are nothing; they are dead. They don't have power — power is our fabrication; it is of our world only; power is not of God's world. Freedom is of God's world and freedom is the opposite of power.

The gospel is the story of how one man who was totally free confronted a world where power is supreme. Pilate said to Jesus, "Do You not know I have *power* to release You and *power* to crucify You?" (Jn 19:11; emphasis added). By denying the power of "the gods" (idols) and instead believing in the true God and in his Sonship to this true God, Jesus was *the one free human.* From appearances, it looked like power won: Jesus was crucified. In reality, freedom won: Jesus was raised.

For us to enter into our freedom as a child of God we must smash our idols. We must deny "the gods" and their power to punish or to judge. We must be willing to leave our illusory world of "the gods," our world of judgment, of guilt and fear. We must be willing to enter into God's world with its commandment: "Do not judge."

Judging

Jesus said, " Do not judge" (Mt 7:1), but just what type of judging was he prohibiting? Certainly we are to make practical judgments. We judge to say "this" rather than "that," "do this," "go there," "work here." We are also required to make moral judgments. We judge some behavior as good, other as bad, some actions life giving, others destructive. Our lives are made up of these practical and moral judgments. Obviously Jesus was not using the word "judge" in these commonly understood ways.

In the New Testament the Greek word that we translate "to judge" literally means to decide, to cut off, or simply to separate. And included in separation is the notion of condemnation and punishment. In Scripture, therefore, the most common understanding of the word "judge" is to separate and condemn. Accordingly, in the New Testament "judge" and "condemn" are used interchangeably. "Do not judge, and you will not be judged" can also be translated "Do not condemn, and you will not be condemned." St. Paul's words "In passing judgment on another you are condemning yourself" (Rm 2:1) can also be said, "In condemning another you are judging yourself." When Jesus said "Do not judge," he was prohibiting judging in this sense of separation and condemnation.

•   •   •   •

We may and indeed must make "judgments" concerning human behavior and the morality of situations; we must "judge" between good and evil. However, in saying this we are not using "judge" in the scriptural,

38

and therefore spiritual, sense. We are not cutting off people or situations. For clarity's sake it may be better to refer to our practical and moral "judgments" as evaluations rather than judgments. We can and must "judge" in the sense of evaluating, but not in the sense of condemning and separating. To make a distinction between evaluation and judgment may seem like idle semantics. But there is a significant difference between "judging" as evaluation and judging as condemnation.

Evaluation accepts life with the good and bad. Condemnation blocks out the bad portions. The first calls for a response, the second for denial. To evaluate a person or situation is to come to terms with it, to accept its existence. To judge is to attempt to reduce that which is to nothing, to cut off existence.

Evaluation is thus discernment, seeing or understanding what is. St. Paul tells us we are "to discern good and evil" (Hb 5:14). Such discernment keeps us in reality and is life giving. On the other hand, judging is deadly, precisely because it separates us from reality.

• • • •

"Faith's name for reality is God." This somewhat startling statement of the Anglican theologian John Macquarrie is not only correct, but also fundamental. It brings home to us the truth that God can be found only in reality and nowhere else. God cannot call us his children in what is not. God can be Father to us only in what is. Our connection with God is our acceptance of reality.

This acceptance does not mean we see bad as good, or wrong as right. It does not mean that we are to be passive or indifferent before life. On the contrary, a true acceptance of life may heighten an awareness of our obligation to change certain situations. Acceptance of reality means simply that we acknowledge that "this is!" Right or wrong, good or bad, "this is!"

It demands that we completely accept the fact that something exists. The necessity of such an acceptance may seem obvious, for what other options do we have? In principle it *is* obvious, but in practice we often avoid acceptance by judging or separating out of reality parts we find distasteful.

As an example of how we are to accept a distasteful reality rather than judge it would be a case like this: Suppose we happen to come across a person being mugged. Naturally we would make a moral "judgment" (evaluation) that "this is evil behavior." Practical "judgments" (evaluations) as to what is to be our response would automatically follow. Our response would vary greatly according to the circumstances. But the point is our evaluations have not separated us from those involved. We can respond without condemning the mugger. Despite what a person does, the person always carries within the dignity of one who is made in God's likeness. Like ourselves, the person is a child of God; at the deepest level we have a bond with the evil-doer, and we cannot deny that unity. If possible, we must stop the evil-doer, using force if necessary, but we cannot pretend that a person is not our brother or sister in Christ. We cannot so judge or cut him off.

•   •   •   •

It is difficult for us to acknowledge that we are not to condemn one who is perpetually evil. In fact, the prohibition against judgment entails something even more difficult. We are not to pretend away the evil-doer, but, moreover, we are not to pretend away or condemn the situation. Again, we evaluate the situation; this means discerning its whole content. The situation exists, is real. Slipping into pretense that it is not an integral part of life (i.e., judging it) frustrates efforts to be wise and effective in responding. Denial in any of its forms makes a response in the Spirit of God impossible. Psychologically it becomes impossible to respond in a life-giving way to a situation when we have condemned it. By our judgment or condemnation we place a barrier between God and the situation so that we are not able to realize that God is here, is present. We are to evaluate an evil situation, not judge it.

There is a familiar example of this in the discoveries about the dynamics of families torn by alcoholism. Often through the psychology of denial, family members condemn or judge the drinking by the alcoholic and cope by counter-productive patterns. Al-Anon and Adult Children of Alcoholics work to help people shed the illusions of denial, their judging and condemning, by helping them see that with a Higher Power [God] we are all bonded together, and that this Higher Power [God] can act in our lives for healing, with our task to be honest and open in seeking healing.

The healing power of these organizations incorporates the realization that neither people nor actions are to be pretended away, or are to be judged, that condemnation is a shortcut to denial, and that by honest discernment we can discover paths to healing. The power of these organizations is that they keep us together in discernment, rather than separated by judgment.

• • • •

When we encounter evil, our feelings will still be aroused, and we will be tempted to condemn. Fear, despair, anger, possibly hatred and hostility are going to surge within us. We may not like the feelings in ourselves. But just as we may not deny the outer reality of people and situations, we may not deny inner realities either. We will be tempted to cut off our feelings of anger, hastily thinking, "I should not feel this way," or "it's not nice to have such feelings." This denial, this condemning, only lets the emotions fester. The feelings have to be accepted, just as everything that is real has to be accepted.

This does not mean that the next step is to give free rein to our anger, hostility or other emotions; it does mean we acknowledge their presence. We may no more deny our personal reality than we can deny external reality. Denial of reality is the essence of judging, for it fosters the illusion of separation. We live with this illusion whenever we attempt to separate ourselves from others, a situation or even ourselves. Such judging is an instance of acting as if something real did not exist.

When Jesus said, "Do not judge," he was prohibiting this attempt to separate what is essentially inseparable, to condemn what in fact exists. He was prohibiting our attempt to deny reality which would be in fact a denial of God.

Should's and Should Not's

There is a mental device we employ whenever we are tempted to deny reality, when we are tempted to judge what is. Mentally we judge or cut off segments of life by thinking, "this should not be." For most of us that phrase, or a variation, is almost a minute-by-minute mantra. "He should not be that way. She should not think that way. That situation should not be. I should not feel this way. Things should be different." All of these bespeak our judgmental minds by which we try to cut off real life and create our version of an ideal world.

Whenever we lay claim to such thoughts as "this should not be," we have entered our world of illusion and thereby denied, or judged, reality. Our "should's" and "should not's" usher us into the make-believe world of "the gods" where everything is right, perfect, good, the way things "should be." To live in our illusory world where we compare "what is" with what "should be" is a type of crippled thinking we have all engaged in. The problem is that irrational behavior is what often follows. When we consider ourselves objectively, it is sometimes amusing; sometimes, though, it is tragic.

A few years ago in the World Series, it appeared as if the St. Louis Cardinals would win the Series in the sixth game against Kansas City. But toward the end of the sixth game, a bad call by the umpire (he himself said later the call was a mistake) led to a Kansas City victory, forcing the Series into a seventh and final game.

Before the seventh game, the St. Louis players were quoted saying, "We should not have lost last night." "We should not be playing tonight." We should be the World Champions." "Right now we should be back in St. Louis celebrating." Reality of course was that they *did* lose game six, they were to play game seven, and they were not world champs celebrating in St. Louis. Mentally, though, the St. Louis team suspended itself somewhere between the reality and their fervent dream of what should be. They had condemned the reality. With one more game to play they had cut themselves off from what was. Denial of loss of the sixth game set in. In a sense, they had separated themselves from existence and so were not fully present in the park at the start of game seven. Kansas City romped them.

It is understandable that St. Louis felt badly about what had happened in that sixth game. But to feel badly about a situation is different from condemning and then denying it. If St. Louis had *evaluated* the previous night's situation instead of condemning or judging it, they would have at least stayed in reality. If they would have said: "Last night the umpire made a bad call and the result was we lost the game... We don't like that, but we can't deny what is. Now how do we respond to the present situation?"

Instead they judged and condemned, they entered the world of "the gods" where everyone is right and perfect, bad things don't exist, and umpires never, ever make a bad call. Such illusory thinking as this "should have been" is destructive.

During and after that seventh game their pitcher and manager were thrown out for cursing and harassing the umpire. Another player mangled his hand by slamming it deliberately into the swirling blades of an electric fan. Still another player took a baseball bat and shattered all the porcelain in the washroom (his best hits of the evening, for which he was fined).

• • • •

These extreme examples show the mental activity which, to a degree, we often indulge in. Aren't we prone to demand a perfect world where our "should's" reign supreme? Aren't we all too ready to condemn people or situations because they are not as they should be, all too ready to deny what is because it does not measure up to the life of "the gods"? And haven't we all experienced the destructiveness of our "should's" and "should not's," the destructiveness of our judging?

Theory vs. Practice
(Thinking vs. Doing)

The "do not judge" of Christianity has a counterpart in a Buddhist saying, "Have a don't-know mind." Both sayings are extremely difficult to explain and seemingly impossibly to practice. How can we not think that something that is wrong should not be? How can we refrain from judging and condemning an evil situation or the offending person?

If we leave Jesus' prohibition on the level of theory we will never answer those questions. Leaving "do not judge" as an abstract principle is to get bogged down in contradictions. "Do not judge" has to be practiced to be understood. To realize what it means we have to live it. It is a manner of doing rather than thinking.

We first have to stop judging, stop condemning, stop separating reality into good and bad. Then and only then will we begin to understand that Our Lord's prohibition against judging is not an impossible command. On the contrary, once we renounce judging we may find that life for us becomes much lighter and easier. "My yoke is easy and my burden light" (Mt 11:30). Are we happy when we are judging? Hardly! As we all know too well, judging is heavy, painful business — pure drudgery!

• • • •

The next time we find ourselves tempted to judge a person or situation, tempted to cut off existence, tempted to think "this should not be" — Stop!

Stop! And instead of judging, let's look at (discern, evaluate) the situation and ask ourselves why we feel so condemnatory and judgmental. If we look deep and honestly enough we will find that our condemnation of another is a projection of our self-condemnation. Persons or situations that we judge as not being as *they* should be, trigger the judgments we have placed on ourselves, because we feel we are not as *we* should be.

Those persons whom we are judging somehow do not measure up to our idols. They are not like our gods. Therefore they are a reminder to us that we feel we have not measured up to our idols, that we are not like our gods. Accordingly, all the judgments, condemnation and punishment we are unconsciously putting on ourselves for not measuring up, we put on them for not measuring up.

Others and situations become for us the arena where we play out our inner sense of guilt and self-punishment. They become the outward sign of our inner division, the whipping boys for the psychological masochism demanded by our self-hatred.

• • • •

Once we accept the fact that our continual judgments of others are rooted in and directed at ourselves, that judging is nothing more than the externalization of our self-judgment, healing can take place. Our healing comes about as we become more and more aware of who we are, children of God, in whom God permanently resides.

God's continual presence within us and his sustaining love for us give us our true identity, so there is no need to condemn and punish ourselves. We need not judge a part of us that we think "should not be," nor condemn ourselves for not measuring up. There is nothing in our identity that we need to deny or cut off.

This being recognized, we will feel no need to deny and cut off others, no need to judge them. Once our self-judging is diffused, our judging of others will slip away quietly. Not that we will be blind to evil, nor impervious to wrongs, but we will have a clearer vision concerning them. With this vision we will see that despite the fact that this person is engaged in evil or this situation is wrong, God is not separate from either. God's love is here, in every person and in every thing.

But it is possible to see and believe in God's presence outside of us only if we first see and believe in God's presence within us. We first have to believe in our oneness with God, our "Abba," to believe that there is not separation between ourselves and God before we can see that neither is God separated from others or situations. For if we don't see God in ourselves we will not see him. If we see God in ourselves, we will see him everywhere, in every situation and in every person.

In this context it may be well to remember that despite the evil of Christ's crucifixion, he never judged the situation or the people involved. He never cut off or denied the reality before him. He never said "this should not be."

Because of our split, good/bad, right/wrong minds, we would have said with St. Peter: "God forbid, Lord, no such thing should ever happen to you" (Mt 16:22) or, "Lord, this *should not* be." Christ never said that because he refused to believe that there was anything in *him* which should not be. For unlike us, he bore no self-hatred, no self-condemnation, no self-judgment, no self-punishment; rather Christ believed "the Father and I are one" (Jn 10:30).

Since Christ believed in his union with God, believed in God's presence in him, he could believe in God's presence outside of him, believe that God is present in *this* reality, in *this* situation, in *these* people. So doing, he lived continually in the kingdom of God.

• • • •

The kingdom of God can always be found in what is in front of our eyes, whether that situation is fraught with evil or not. And in this kingdom, God does not ask why things are as they are, but "What is your response to the way things are?" We can never make a response to the way things are if we are continually thinking "Why should this be?"

Since the "why" of life is not central in the kingdom, the Buddhist saying of having a "don't-know mind" has sense to it; we are to respond with discernment that includes seeing God's presence in every situation, and not to freeze ourselves in railing against reality.

With our response to reality we enter the kingdom. Crossing that threshold, we leave our split selves and judgments behind. We enter the Wholeness God offers us; we enter into God's world.

Part Two

God's World

The ordinary human brain thinks in terms of duality; light and darkness, sweet and sour, good and evil. That duality does not exist in nature [in God's world].[1]

Jesus told us "the Kingdom of God is not of this world" (Jn 18:36), but by saying that, he was not saying the kingdom of God is some place else. No, God's world is right here. (Mk 1:15) The kingdom of God, or God's world, is right before us but it does not conform to the divided world we have created. Our world is really no world at all; it is a pseudo world based on our illusion of separation.

Our world is the result of original sin, of our eating of the dualistic tree of the knowledge of good and evil. "From *that* tree you shall not eat; the moment you eat of it, you are surely doomed to die" (Gn 2:17). We ate; we judged, condemned and punished. We died.

But that picture was not left totally bleak. "Good News" eventually came. The good news of the gospel proclaimed that our illusory world of judgment, separation, and death is not God's world. God's world lies beyond the split world we have made by dividing reality into "what is good and what is evil."

In the Genesis story, besides the tree of the knowledge of good and evil, there is another tree of note: "the tree of life, in the middle of the garden..." (Gn 2:9). In contrast to the tree of the knowledge of good and evil that we choose, this tree of life has only one part. It is not a dualistic tree of life and death, but a simple tree of life. The tree of life has no

---

[1]Irving Stone, *Lust for Life* (New York: New American Library, 1934), p. 337.

parts, no division, no separation, so it can have no opposites, no alienation. It excludes condemnation because it excludes judgment.

God's world, symbolized by the tree of life, is a world of unity,
simplicity, oneness (and it is "very good"; Gn 1:31). And when God had
created it, he "looked at everything He had made, and found it very good"
(Gn 1:31). This "good" which God speaks over *all* creation is not the
"good" of our good vs. bad dualism. It is not the human good which required an opposite.

The "good" which God speaks over creation is the "good" of being
itself, of which there is no opposite. It is the "good" of existence which
includes the presence of God. This "good" means "is." When God said,
"it is good," he was saying: "it is," and nothing is opposite to "is." *"Is"*
is good because "isness," like God himself, is utterly one, is totally simple. God's world is made up of the simple good. Our world is made up
of good *and* bad.

It is no wonder, then, with our dualistic mind by which we know
good and bad, we can't understand God's world of only "the good." God's
world is one of wholeness "and it is good." Our world is one of division:
"this is good, *that* is bad." God's world has no judgment; our world has
constant judgment. God's world consisted only of what is; our world
consists of what is *and* what *is not.* God's world makes no sense to our
mind.

The "human brain which thinks in terms of duality" could not even
imagine God's world unless another revealed it to us. That revealer is
Jesus Christ, and "He testifies to what He has seen and heard" (Jn 3:32).

Parables and Leaven

Christ revealed God's world to us. And to make sure we "got the point," he usually began with "the kingdom of God is like..." Then he went on to tell a parable. These parables are riddles that were intended to "blow" our judgmental minds and thus our world apart, that is, *if* we would let them. Too often, however, we just turn the parables into morality stories, good vs. bad, right vs. wrong, and fit these doublets into our dualistic world view. Instead of allowing the parables to reveal God's world we use them to make sense in our world.

So the parables don't change our mind as Christ intended them to. Like the people who first heard them, we "have eyes but no sight, ears but no hearing..." (Mk 8:18). The parables do not conform to our world view, to our model of what should or should not be.

In this sense, the parables are like that leaven that Christ spoke about when he said "the kingdom of God is like leaven which a woman took and hid in three measures of flour" (Mt 13:33 Douay). We don't get the full impact of that statement because for us leaven has a very different connotation than it had for the ancient peoples.

Since they did not understand leaven they saw it as something mysterious and sinister; they felt somewhat threatened by it. Like black magic, leaven conjured up thoughts of dark and unknown forces. Its effects could be seen but it was not known how these effects came about. To the people of Christ's time leaven had a negative association; it suggested something evil or at least something that was not as it "should be." It was this negative sense that Christ was suggesting when he said: "Beware of the *leaven* of the Pharisees and of the *leaven* of Herod" (Mk

8:15). When he said that the kingdom of God is like leaven he was telling us that the kingdom can be immersed in negative circumstances.

The kingdom of God may even appear to us as something bad. It may be present in what we think "should not be." We continually meet situations, events and people whom we judge as not being as they "should be." They seem to us to be wrong, bad or even evil.

Christ, by saying that the kingdom is like leaven, is telling us that the kingdom of God is present even in the midst of these negative situations. He is telling us that God is present in what appears to us to be wrong, is present in those situations we think "should not be." The parables stress this same point; that God is present in "bad" situations, in "bad" people.

The parables, then, are "leaven stories." They threaten our way of thinking and judging. They turn upside down our judgment, our reason, our logic. We hear the parables and we automatically make negative judgments: "This isn't right. It's not what it should be. That is wrong."

Yet Christ is telling us the kingdom of God is like "that"; is like the prodigal son, the good Samaritan, the late workers in the vineyard, etc. God is present in what disturbs and upsets us, in what we want to deny. The kingdom of God is like those things and those people whom we judge negatively.

It is clear from the parables that the kingdom of God destroys our standard for judgment. It is the prodigal son, the irresponsible, dissipating son, who gets the reward of the banquet, not the dutiful homebody. In the good Samaritan story, the hero is not a good person (symbolized by the people who passed by) but a bad person (symbolized by the Samaritan who helped). *All* the workers in the vineyard, the lazy ones who arrived late as well as the industrious early risers, receive the same pay.

Where does our standard for judgment fit into these parables? It doesn't! Where does our sense of fairness fit into these parables? It doesn't! Where is the logic in them? There isn't any!

Is it reasonable to leave the ninety-nine sheep to the danger of predators and go off to find the one who got lost, and who very likely is by now dead? That's not reasonable! These parables tell us that there is no reason or logic in the kingdom of God.

Only minds that can separate and divide can speak reasonably and logically. Since God's mind can't separate, he doesn't speak reasonably by human standards and he doesn't speak logically. This is why Christ had to describe God's kingdom by parables. To use stark rhetoric demands human reason and logic, two attributes God does not have.

Injustice

Just as our reason and logic have no part in God's world, neither does justice. Besides revealing what the kingdom of God is like, Christ also told us how to live in that kingdom.

> You have heard the commandment, "an eye for an eye, a tooth for a tooth!" But what I say to you is: offer no resistance to injury. When a person strikes you on the right cheek, turn and offer him the other. If anyone wants to go to law over your tunic [let him have it and] give him your cloak as well. Should anyone press you into service for one mile, go with him two miles… You have heard the commandment, "You shall love your countryman but hate your enemy." My commandment to you is: love your enemies, pray for your persecutors. (Mt 5:38–44)

If that is what living in God's world is like, where is justice? In our world, if we are assaulted we don't turn the other cheek. We fight back, at the very least, demanding restitution and damages for injuries. That is the justice that holds society together.

And who in our world ever heard of acquiescing before an unjust lawsuit, and then giving our adversary *more* than what he is suing for — the tunic *plus* the cloak. Such "Godly" foolishness would crumble our legal system.

Also it is very *unjust* to pay those workers in the vineyard (Mt 20:1–16), who labored ten hours in the day's heat, the very same pay that is given to those who worked only one hour in the cool of the evening. Justice demands "an honest day's wage for an honest day's work." That is the justice that keeps our economic system functioning. And any making of "the last to be first and the first last" (Mt 20:16) would utterly destroy that system.

It is obvious from the way that Christ described the kingdom of God that humankind's justice is absent in that kingdom. To our way of thinking, this makes the kingdom very unjust. As Martin Luther said, "If you follow human reason [i.e., human justice], you are forced to say either there is no God, or that God is unjust...."[2]

We can't predicate justice of God because our idea of justice is not applicable to the nature of God. "If God's justice were such as could be adjudged just by human reckoning, it clearly would not be Divine; it would in no way differ from human justice. But inasmuch as God is wholly incomprehensible... His 'justice' also should be incomprehensible."[3]

Justice demands that perpetrators of injustice pay for the offenses committed. In our world offenses have to be rectified, offenses have to be balanced on the scales of justice. But there is no such thing as human justice in the kingdom of God precisely because in God's world there is no such thing as an offense.

---

[2]Martin Luther, "Bondage of the Will," as quoted in John Dillenberger, *Martin Luther* (Garden City, N.Y.: Doubleday and Co., 1961), p. 201.
[3]Ibid., p. 200.

Forgiveness Is Non-Judgment

Christ revealed that the kingdom of God does not conform to our model of judgment by which we continually divide, judging some as good, others as bad, including some as acceptable, excluding others as unacceptable. "Whenever you give a dinner, do not invite your friends..." (Lk 14:12).

Division of others into friends and enemies is only our doing. In reality there is no such division. No one can be our enemy unless we have first judged him to be offensive. But an offense is something that occurs only in our judgmental mind. No one could offend us if we weren't first an offense to ourselves. No one could oppose us if we were not in opposition to ourselves. Offenses and enemies make up our world of guilt and self-punishment. In God's world there can be no enemies because no offense is every taken. And if there are no offenses there is nothing to forgive.

That is the point of our Lord's words that if someone offends us we should "forgive them seventy times seven times" (Mt 18:22). To take that literally would be impossible. Is it possible to continually forgive someone whom we judge to be continually attacking and abusing us? To repeatedly forgive what we have judged to be a repeated offense is impossible because we are starting from the wrong mind-set. We have first judged, "This is an offense against us"; and *that* very act of judging or condemning shows we don't have the mind of God.

It is not a question of our judging people (that's our world) and then forgiving them seventy times seven times. It is a question of not judging the person at all (that's God's world). "Do not judge" (Mt 7:2).

In effect, forgiving someone seventy times seven times (continual or unlimited forgiveness) means eliminating all judgment in the first place, so that there is nothing to forgive. It is as if Christ is saying: "Don't even make a judgment that the other has wronged you." If we do, we are not in God's world. Our very act of judging another shows that we are in our own world of inner division and that we are acting out of our dualistic illusion of good/bad, right/wrong. If we do judge we are merely projecting onto another our internal split, our self-condemnation.

This is why Christ said, "the judgments you give are the judgments you will get" (Mt 7:2 JB). He does *not* mean that if we judge someone, God will judge us. Rather the very judgment we are giving another is the judgment we are making on ourselves. We are getting from ourselves our own judgment. We are placing on another what we have first placed on ourselves.

When we judge others we are merely externalizing our internal division where our false self is judging our true self. Our idealized image (what we think we should be) is judging who we really are and saying that we are bad, wrong and not what we "should be." Our self-condemnation then becomes the condemnation of others and we say *they* are bad, wrong, not what *they* should be. We have seen ourselves in others and have judged them as we judge ourselves.

Christ said that if we make the ultimate judgment, the ultimate division, and say to another "you fool," we shall be liable to hell's fire (Mt 5:22). Again this does not mean God will judge us and condemn us to hell; rather he is telling us that our act of going against another is going against ourselves. God will not punish us for calling another a fool. We are punishing ourselves when we call another a fool.

Our judging of another is the outward manifestation of our inward separation, our inner contradiction. Half of us is moving against, attacking or punishing the other half and that hurts. That self-alienation tears us apart and that burns. *That* is the hell fire Christ is talking about.

When we judge we are acting out of our personal hell, the hell of self-punishment that we inflict on ourselves because we feel guilty for not being as we should be. The judgment of hell fire is a present condition we are putting on ourselves, not a future condition put on us by God. Christ said, "whoever does not believe is already condemned [judged]" (Jn 3:18).

Our lack of belief in Christ as our identity, as who we truly are, our lack of belief in our oneness, our wholeness, is already a judgment against ourselves; it is already our hell. We are alienated, separated, cut off, "judged" from our true self. But we are the ones creating that judgment, creating that hell, no one else, not even and especially not God.

"Stop judging and you will not be judged." "Do not judge and you will not be judged" (Lk 6:37 JB). From these words of Christ it is apparent that judging is all our doing; it begins and ends with us.

God's only purpose is to save. We are the ones who judge and condemn, separate and cut off, and this judgment is now; *we* make our own "judgment day," a self-imposed present reality. (See the New American Bible note for Jn 3:17–19: "Some judge *themselves* by turning from the light.")

We initiate and receive our own judgment although those around us may feel the fallout. For judgment is not placed on us from the outside; it comes from within and is in our hands; we are the ones who control it.

We can hold onto it, or we can drop it. If we hold onto it, we give judgment existence. If we drop it, judgment has no existence. "Stop judging and you will not be judged."

It's a sobering thought, fraught with responsibility, to realize that God has nothing to do with judging. Rather it is only through us that judgment can possibly enter the world. God does not judge! We do! That realization is frightening.

Judging and all that goes with it — guilt, fear, punishment, death, hell, devils — make up *our* world, not God's. "God is not the God of the dead but of the living, for to Him all are alive" (Lk 20:38). Ours is a world we create whenever we judge, whenever we are internally split or divided.

"Do not judge." To judge rightly or wrongly is irrelevant; to judge another or ourselves is also irrelevant. Simply do not judge. If we do, we are eating from the tree of good and bad, rather than from the tree of life. Christ also often said, "Forgive." "Do not judge" and "Forgive." The two are the same.

Forgiveness means non-judgment. Otherwise it would be a contradiction to be told, "Do not judge" and "Forgive." We have to judge in order to forgive. We can't forgive something we haven't judged to be wrong. Our Lord's words, "Do not judge" and "Forgive" are synonymous. Forgiveness means there is no judgment, i.e., no separation nor condemnation in the first place.

The "Unforgiving" Francis

There is a story concerning St. Francis of Assisi which illustrates the principle that since forgiveness is non-judgment, forgiveness becomes insignificant; or to put it more succinctly, true forgiveness is not!

Francis' story is disturbing because in it he describes how it would be "pure joy" if someone would attack, abuse, humiliate and insult him. It is only disturbing to us, however, because we focus on the wrong part of the story. We focus on the offense, at Francis' discomfort and humiliation, while the saint is concerned only with his response to the offense. Francis is not saying he takes delight in pain or insults, but he is saying that to be free from judging even when being attacked is our greatest joy. The story is about inner freedom not about external abuse; and this freedom more than compensates for any abuse which may come our way. "Pure joy" resides in that freedom that cannot be offended or insulted.

Francis knew that we could not be insulted or offended if we were not insulting or offensive to ourselves. So if we are being attacked by another and yet do not feel insulted, we know we are accepting and loving ourselves. To refuse to judge another who is harming us is a sign that we are not judging ourselves. Not to judge, attack or insult ourselves is the great freedom, the great joy. And the test for this freedom and joy is how we react to offensive behavior. At those times it is not a question of what the other is doing to us; what we are doing to ourselves is the determining factor.

To use a more contemporary example: A star football player such as Joe Montana would not be the least bit insulted or offended if someone told him he was the worst quarterback who ever played the game. Because he has not so judged himself, it would be impossible to take those words seriously. Therefore, any talk of his "forgiving the speaker" would be absurd. His identity as a great quarterback is too secure for anyone to threaten it. On the other hand, an insecure fourteen-year-old could be very insulted and offended by those words, and it would be difficult for such a youngster to forgive the offender.

In Francis' story, he never mentions forgiving the offender. He is totally "unforgiving" because he is not concerned with the offense. Francis' identity as a child of God is too secure for anyone to threaten it. Knowing himself to be a son of his heavenly Father and a brother to all living beings, nothing anyone did to him could diminish the presence of God in his life. Since he takes no offense, no forgiveness is possible. Francis is telling us that true Christian forgiveness is really non-judgment and in non-judgment lies our peace and joy. Our "forgiving" offenders "seventy times seven times" is automatic when we are free from self-judgment. When we refrain from judging and hurting ourselves, when we are secure in our own identity, another can't hurt us. Then judging and forgiving another becomes unthinkable because there is nothing to judge and therefore nothing to forgive.

St. Francis' total acceptance of himself, his total love of himself in God, which is his humility, may be beyond us. But hopefully we can at least have his ability to see that when another attacks or insults us, the real problem is not in what the other person is doing to us but in what we are doing to ourselves. The real problem is that we are our own judge and hangman. No one else can assume those roles against us unless we first, by judging ourselves, give them the power to do so.

God Doesn't Judge

Since judgment and punishment are so much a part of our world we continually read them into the gospels. Our bifocal vision of good/bad is so much in our mind that we impose it onto Christ's mind. We even call one thief on Calvary "good" and the other one "bad." Christ didn't! He didn't turn to the one, saying: "And you won't be with me in Paradise, because you are bad."

We automatically make that assumption because we think in contrasts. We just assume the good/bad dichotomy because we see ourselves in terms of that dualism. Then we fit everything and everyone into our framework of judgment. Situations are satisfactory or unsatisfactory; the world is divided into good people and bad people.

We should realize that it is we who are making those divisions, those judgments and neither God nor Christ is caught up with our split thinking. Judging is so much a part of our world that it is extremely difficult for us to relate to a God who does not judge.

Most Christians, if told that God does not judge, would object. Yet Christ said plainly, "The Father judges no one..." (Jn 5:22). St. Paul repeats this truth, stressing that God, rather than passing judgment on us, sets us free: "If God is for us, who can be against us?" (Rm 8:31). "It is God Who acquits us, who will condemn [judge]?" (Rm 8:33–34).

When we consider who God is and what judging is, we see that it is impossible to think of God in terms of judging, for the two ideas are contradictory.

St. John says simply "God is love" (I Jn 4:8). This means that God is loving *all* the people *all* the time. This unconditional love precludes any type of judgment. Unconditional Love (God) can't cut anyone off, can't separate some and say, "You are unworthy of my love." To so judge would deny the unconditional aspect of Divine Love. God didn't judge Adolph Hitler to be less lovable than any of the saints. God didn't (doesn't) love Hitler less than the Little Flower (St. Theresa of Lisieux).

Since Divine Love is by its very nature universal and unlimited, it can't decide (literally, "cut off") among its recipients; Love Itself can't divide humanity into lovable and unlovable. When Scripture says that "God is love," it is saying "God can't judge." For to judge something is to place it outside of us. But there is nothing outside of God's love.

An equally significant reason God can't judge is that God is pure Light. "God is light and in Him there is no darkness" (I Jn 1:5). God who is total Light within can't divide into darkness without. Being internally undifferentiated God can't externally differentiate. Since God is Being Itself and Being has no parts, God can't "think" in terms of or know parts.

Indivisible Light is incompatible with division, Unmitigated Light with separation. Universal Light doesn't have an alternative or opposite. So when Scripture says "God is Light" or "God is love," it is telling us "God can't judge."

Who God is, Light and Love, places God at variance with any notion of judging. The very nature of God — unconditional, total, complete — is opposed to the nature of judging — dividing, cutting-off, separating. For God to cut off, differentiate, separate would necessitate that God deny his own being, deny who he is. Such a denial would be a contradiction in terms.

From what has been said, it is apparent that God, unconditional Love and Unimpaired Light, is beyond understanding. A God in whom there is no division or judgment is incomprehensible to our thoughts and ways. "My thoughts are not your thoughts. Nor are your ways My ways, says the Lord. As high as the heavens are above the earth so are My ways above your ways and My thoughts above your thoughts" (Is 55:8–9).

And this Old Testament incomprehension before the mystery of God continues into the New Testament. "Who has known the mind of God? ...How unsearchable His ways" (Rm 11:33–34). Then St. Paul adds: "How unsearchable His judgments"; and we know that God's judgments are unsearchable precisely because — they aren't!

In reality there is no such thing as the judgment of God. For if God could judge, God wouldn't be God. Unity would cause division. Love Itself would have an opposite. Accordingly, "God did not send His Son into the world to judge [condemn] the world but that the world might be saved through Him" (Jn 3:17).

Possibly the most conclusive indication that God doesn't judge is the most obvious one — the fact that Christ told us not to judge. Would Christ forbid us to do something his Father does? Would he tell us *not* to do something which is in fact a Godly act?

If God does judge, would not Christ have told us also to judge? We know that Christ wanted us to be God-like. Indeed he told us to be more than just God-like; he told us, "Be perfect as your heavenly Father is perfect" (Mt 5:48). The phrase "be perfect" is misleading because the biblical meaning of "perfect" is complete or whole. In contemporary English, however, "perfect" carries the additional meaning of flawless, or absolutely unblemished. If we take "perfect" in this English sense we could very easily end up a compulsive perfectionist, forever trying for the impossible. Or else we would despair in the face of the demand; how could we ever be as perfect as God?

Of all the evangelists, only Matthew (for reasons we will see later) ever uses the word "perfect." The parallel account in Luke reads, "Be merciful as your Heavenly Father is merciful" (Lk 6:36). So the Matthean word "perfect" is equivalent to God's mercy or God's love as Luke so relates it. God's "perfection" (that is, his completeness or wholeness) resides then in his universal love of humankind.

Matthew, like Luke, does equate perfection with God's universal love. But he does it by way of everyday examples. He says the Father "makes His sun rise on the bad and the good, causes His rain to fall on the just and unjust" (Mt 5:45). This saying is an example of Luke's merciful God. Both evangelists are saying the same thing, that God doesn't cut anyone off from his love. With God there is no differentiation; both the good and bad receive his blessings of sun and rain. He does not separate peoples. He relates to the just and the unjust in the same manner. For "[God] is kind to the ungrateful and the wicked" (Lk 6:35). The Father of our Lord Jesus Christ, our Father, is unique precisely in that *he is kind to the wicked!* That is the distinctive characteristic of the Christian God: He loves those who from our perspective are not deserving of love. It is no wonder that it is in this passage that we find the hardest of Christ's commands: "Love your enemies" (Mt 5:44).

That command is the principle of universal love carried to its logical yet extreme conclusion, depicted as the sun and rain falling on all, friends and enemies. Christ is telling us that God does not cut off, does not separate, which is, as we have seen, equivalent to saying God does not judge. Our heavenly Father does not divide humankind and say "the good people are eligible to receive my blessings; the bad people are not."

Bright sunny days and soft spring rain fall on both Al Capone and Chicago's Little Sisters of the Poor. Since *we* are internally split (judgmental) we do not like that arrangement at all, but God, who is internally whole (non-judgmental) lives with it quite well.

Since time began God has been bestowing the same means of sustenance, sun and rain, on the bad and good with total disregard to individuals and their behavior. All people benefit from God's goodness. All are recipients of his love. Therein lies his perfection which we can and are to imitate.

Christ's command "to be perfect as your heavenly Father is perfect" is not as impossible as it appears at first glance. To be like God is to relate to all as he does. We are to judge no one, exclude none from our good will. We, like God, are to let our blessings, *our* sun and rain, fall on the good and the bad alike, that is, we are to have a love which is complete and whole. Implied in such an unlimited love is that we first overcome our internal dividedness and so enter into our personal wholeness. "Be holy, for I, the Lord your God am Holy" (Lv 20:7). Or, be whole, for I, the Lord your God am whole. Be not divided!

To the degree we accept our personal wholeness and then extend this completeness to all others indiscriminately (wholly), to that degree we will be perfect as our heavenly Father is perfect. We will be loving as God is loving.

We have seen that both Scripture and reason tell us that God, being unconditional love, cannot judge or punish. Why then does our idea of God as judge so persistently stay with us as individuals and communities?

I think that one of the main reasons the idea of God as judge appeals to us stems from a faulty perception not only of ourselves, as people deserving of punishment, but also of creation.

Our divided view of creation is not the same as God's undivided creation as we will see in the next chapter.

Part Three

Two Creations

In God's kingdom, in his world, in his creation, there is no negativity, no evil and no sin. In Genesis there are two creation stories. In the first story (Gn 1:3–2:4), creation, or the world, is seen from God's perspective. In this first account, the way that God sees it, he created everything including humankind and "finds it good." To emphasize this goodness of creation, "It is good" is repeated after every act of creation. "And God saw that...it was good." This version concludes with "God looked at everything he had made, and he found it very good" (Gn 1:31).

In this story, "good" is spoken by God seven times, the perfect number. There are no flaws in creation from God's viewpoint. When God said that all of creation was good, that was it! The creator never changed his mind about the goodness of creation, including the goodness of humankind. And since God is always creating and creation is always a present event, God is saying *right now,* "It is very good." *Now* God looks at everything and says "It is good." *Now* God looks at every person and says, "He or she is good." Creation from God's perspective is good *now;* it contains no negativity or evil because there is no negativity or evil in God.

The second creation story (Gn 2:5–3:21) is presented from the human perspective. It is how *we* see creation. Since we see negativity in ourselves, we see creation and the world in negative terms. Having eaten of the tree of good and evil and having believed the tempter who said "you will be like gods who know what is good and what is bad" (Gn 3:5), we "know" evil and we "see" the bad in creation. What we know (evil) colors our perspective so that nowhere in this second story — *our* story — is creation said to "be good."

73

There are some good things present in the second story: trees "delightful to look at and good for food" (Gn 2:9), but nowhere is there pronounced "It is good." We see creation as a reflection of ourselves whom we see as bad. Creation through our perspective as distinct from God's has everything tinged with evil. In our notion of creation is found elements of fear and punishment stemming from feelings of guilt. Since whenever we feel guilty we will project our feelings onto others and say "they are guilty," our story abounds in projection with everyone seeing others as bad.

Adam projects his sense of guilt onto Eve: "she gave me fruit" (Gn 3:12); the woman is bad! Eve projects her sense of guilt onto the serpent: "the serpent tricked me…" (Gn 3:13); the serpent is bad! The story ends with both Adam and Eve projecting their negativity on God. "God is bad!" They felt that they were bad so they transferred their feelings to God and God became a "bad God." They in fact turn the true God into "the gods" who talk very negatively among themselves (Gn 3:22ff). "See! The man has become like one of us.…he must not be allowed to…live forever."

God is seen as getting jealous of humanity (a projection of human jealousy of divine power). God is seen as wanting to deprive humans of life. Humans "must not be allowed to live forever" (a projection of our desire to steal God's life). God separates himself from humans. God "banished"; God "expelled"; God "set a guard." There are projections of our feelings of being separated from God, of being divided and blocked from union with God.

In our version of creation we turn God into the punitive "gods." We transpose our need for self-punishment to God, making our loving Father who sees only the good into a punitive God who punishes the bad.

God Doesn't Know Evil

From our perspective we see a part of creation as bad; we see evil. We know the negative that is present in ourselves and in our world. We know sin! But that is not God's perspective! That is not how he sees creation or humankind. God doesn't see the negative. The "non-good" is not in his vision, for to him it is always "very good." Accordingly, God sees neither sin nor evil.

Evil is defined in Christian theology as the absence of good: *privatio boni.*

St. Thomas Aquinas said that "Evil is not a being"; it is "distinct from being because it is a privation." Since it is essentially non-being, "evil implies an absence of good."[1] St. Augustine likewise defined evil as "a *privation* of mode, species and order,"[2] "the *nonentity* which is called *evil.*"[3]

God can't know an absence or lack. God can't see what isn't; he can't know or see what doesn't exist, i.e., non-being or a privation of being.

God is Being; sin is non-being. Being can have no connection with non-being. If sin had being, God, who is Being Itself, would have to be its cause. Non-being, nothing, unreality, darkness, a void, a lack — these are all synonyms for sin. It is impossible for God to know any of

---

[1] St. Thomas Aquinas, *Summa Theologica,* translated by the Fathers of the English Dominican Province, Great Books of the Western World, vols. 19–20 (Chicago: William Benton Publisher, 1952), 19:261.

[2] Ibid., 20:18; emphasis added.

[3] St. Augustine, *The Fathers of the Church,* vol. 1 (New York: Cima Publishing Co., 1948), p. 199; emphasis added.

these nonentities. Reality can't know unreality or fullness a void. Light cannot know darkness.

When Scripture speaks of evil it does not use philosophical language such as non-being or non-existence. But Scripture, like philosophy, often portrays evil as a privation or absence.

A major biblical theme is the contrast between light (symbolizing good) and darkness (symbolizing evil). The episode of Judas exiting the Last Supper to betray Jesus concludes with the chilling words "and it was night" (Jn 13:30). Darkness prevailed! When Jesus was arrested in the garden of Gethsemani, he said that now is "the time for the power of darkness" (Lk 22:53).

Jesus often used physical darkness or a lack of light to describe spiritual darkness or a lack of good. "Whoever follows Me will not walk in darkness" (Jn 8:12).

Symbolically, evil was also associated with blindness and sickness — blindness being an absence of sight, and sickness being an absence of health. But Christ overcame these privations, these evils, by his light and truth. Light and truth are of being. Evil is of non-being. By its very nature, evil or sin is nothing. We mistakenly believe this nothing is something because we see the effects of evil.

But if evil were something it would have existence and God would have to be within it. If sin had existence, God would have to be its cause.

Dostoevsky in *The Brothers Karamazof* has the devil described as "the spirit of self-destructiveness and non-existence."[4] But God who is Existence Itself can know nothing of non-existence. The Eternal Is — is incompatible with what is not.

To say that God sees sin makes no more sense than to say that we can look into a dark hole and see something. There is nothing there to see! Sin is only in our vision of the world in our version of the creation story. It is not in God's creation story nor in his vision. God does not know sin.

---

[4]Dostoevsky, *The Brothers Karamazof,* p. 130.

Two fourteenth-century mystics, Blessed Julian of Norwich and the Dominican, Meister Eckhart, spoke of sin or evil as follows: "I believe that [sin] has no kind of substance, no share in being, nor can it be recognized except by the pain it causes."[5] "Evil as non-being is not from God, nor is God in it, since there is no existence in it...this is why it does not exist."[6]

But what does it mean to say "sin is a privation, an absence"; "sin has no share in being"; "evil does not exist"? What does it mean to say sin is a "nonentity"?

When we see a child caught in an abusive, brutal home, aren't we seeing the existence of evil? Looking at the death camps, sin definitely seems to be something. To deny that evil has existence in the face of such human destructiveness and pain approaches blasphemy. Besides, Christ spoke about sins; was he speaking about something that has no existence?

To understand why Sin or Evil is said to have no substance, no being, we have to distinguish between "Sin" and "sins." The distinction is that there is a difference between Evil and the manifestation of evil, namely the thoughts, words and deeds, those situations and structures which are obviously sinful.

Sin or Evil is non-being because it resides in a perceived separation from God. But we are not really separated from God, so the "Evil" is not real; in Augustine's words, it is a "nonentity." Evil is the illusion that we are split off from our Source. Because it is an illusion, Evil has no existence, no reality of its own.

Nevertheless we can respond to this illusory gap, to non-being in devastating ways. We can turn evil or sin, which is nothing, into sins which are something. We can allow the illusion of separation to have effects on our lives. And those damaging effects are sins.

---

[5]*Julian of Norwich, "Showings"* translated by Edmund Colledge and James Walsh, Classics of Western Spirituality (New York: Paulist Press, 1978), p. 148.

[6]*Meister Eckhart: Teacher and Preacher,* translated by Edmund Colledge and Bernard McGinn, Classics of Western Spirituality (Mahwah, N.J.: Paulist Press, 1986), p. 152.

The sins are real, by them we can destroy ourselves. So the effects of sin are very real but sin or evil itself is nothing.

The spiritual classic *The Scale of Perfection* (c. 1380) summed up the traditional understanding of sin: "What is sin? ...Indeed it is nothing... This nothing is no other than a *lack* of love and light, as sin is but an *absence* of good."[7]

---

[7]*Walter Hilton, "The Scale of Perfection,"* translated by John P. H. Clark and Rosemary Dorward, Classics of Western Spirituality (Mahwah, N.J.: Paulist Press, 1986), p. 124; emphasis added.

Illusion and Guilt

Sin, or non-being, is rooted in the illusion that we are separate from God. Most people, if asked the whereabouts of God, would instinctively point toward the sky or possibly to a church. Even though they probably would deny they mean it literally, this pointing to God as outside of themselves is significant. Their pointing elsewhere expresses a belief in a distance between themselves and God. Another manifestation of our imagined separation from God is the feeling that we have within us a void or space. This space also creates a distance between ourselves and God. For therein lies all the things we think we should not be. It is the home of our false self.

Here resides the most devastating result of our illusion of separation, an all-pervasive sense of guilt. We feel guilty about an inner space that is not there. We feel guilty about a void which does not exist, guilt about an imaginary distance. Guilt is the glue which holds all this unreality together. Guilt keeps our illusions intact.

• • • •

Guilt and our illusion of separation are so closely connected it is difficult to distinguish which comes first. Is it our sense of guilt that gives rise to the feeling of separation between ourselves and God, or is it our sense of separation that gives rise to our sense of guilt?

I do not know, but I suspect it is like the question of the chicken or the egg. For our purposes, we will start with the premise that it is our illusion of separation that gives rise to our sense of guilt.

Guilt is the *result* of feeling we are separated from God. Our sense of guilt in turn demands that we move against, or punish, ourselves. Another name for self-punishment is self-alienation. We are in the grip of self-alienation when one part of us judges or punishes another part of us, when one half hates the other half. And this judging of ourselves, this self-alienation, is manifested in thoughts, words and deeds.

These are our sins! Sins are the ways we act out our inner division and self-punishment. It appears that others are the primary targets for our sins, but in fact our sins are always self-directed.

The path through which we move from *sin* to *sins,* through guilt and self-alienation, is this: Sin is the belief that we are separated from God, a belief that has no basis in reality. In order for the unreality (sin) to occur we must first turn the true God into one of "the gods." We must make God an idol.

Since an idol has no existence, when we believe we are separated from an idol we, by our very belief, enter into the idol's non-existence. When we imagine we are separated from "something" that is unreal we ourselves are caught up in that something's unreality. Being caught up in unreality does have a *real* effect on our lives, and the effect is guilt!

Guilt and idols go together. You cannot have idols without guilt, and you cannot have guilt without idols. Since there is no separation between ourselves and the true God, any guilt we feel because of a supposed separation must be guilt before the false gods, that is, idols.

Anytime we experience a sense of guilt because we feel a distance between ourselves and God, we have turned the living God into "the gods." We have made God an idol and our relationship to him is idolatrous. No wonder Merton said, "idolatry *was,* and *is,* the fundamental sin."[8]

Idolatry is what original sin is all about. We create "the gods" and then desire (concupiscence) to be like them: "you shall be like the gods." This is why original sin has been associated with concupiscence (desire). Of course we cannot live up to unreal desires, so guilt, self-hate and punishment are inevitable.

---

[8]See p. 13 above; emphasis added.

To summarize: Sin is a belief in a fictional separation, which separation is founded on idolatry. The first result of *sin* is guilt. Guilt then leads to self-alienation and self-alienation leads to *sins*.

Hopefully, an example can help us see, at least in an analogous way, the line between *sin* and *sins*: Suppose there is a painter who is recognized by all to be the world's greatest living artist. But for some reason the painter himself cannot recognize the greatness of his art. He does not recognize who he is. He feels a void in his ability, a feeling there is a lack of artistic talent within him. He feels there is a separation, a distance, between what he is as an artist and what he should be. In fact, the acclaim he receives from others only intensifies the artist's sense of falling short.

His idea that he is devoid of all artistic ability is pure illusion, but he firmly believes it. Moreover, he feels very guilty about the separation he sees between the artist as he envisions himself and the idols, the "artistic gods," of his imagination. Since he is trying to measure up to idols he is bound to feel inferior. Regardless of how talented he is, when he compares himself to an idol, he can never be good enough, and the only possible consequence is a feeling of guilt. This sense of guilt leads him to self-alienation or self-punishment.

The most common way the artist's inner-alienation will show itself is in his relationships toward anyone who is a reminder of the hatred he feels toward himself. Most likely, therefore, his fellow artists would receive the brunt of his sense of guilt. Since, in his mind, they, like himself, could never live up to his idols, they would serve as reminders to him of just how guilty he feels before those idols.

Seeing that they are not what *they should be* would surface his unconscious feelings that he is not what *he should be*. The other artists would then naturally become the objects of his inner-alienation and self-hatred. The guilt-ridden artist would see other artists as guilty and so project his self-punishment onto them. He would move against them with anger, ridicule, insults, all the ways we punish others by thoughts, words and deeds.

These thoughts, words and deeds are his *sins,* his self-punishment projected onto others. These sins have their beginning in his *sin*, his illusion of separation from God. The latter (sin) or evil does not really exist. The former (sins) do exist, and their effects are painful, even devastating.

The Pain of Sins

Like the artist's, our sins are also attempts to fill up a space that is not there. We wrongly feel we lack something so we desire to fill up that lack. Not knowing we are children of the true God, we desire to be like the false gods. This illusory desire, or concupiscence, leads to sins. "Hatred, strife, envy, fear, wrath, sorrow and similar things arise from the lack of something *desired*."[9]

Every one of our sins is a compensatory activity. We desire to compensate for a felt lack. Traditionally this desire has been categorized into the seven capital sins. There are seven different categories by which we attempt to close that imaginary gap (a lack) between ourselves and God. Each of these sins is in its own way an effort to eliminate a fictional separation between who we are, human beings, and who we think we should be, one of the gods:

Avarice — that desire to get more of something: money, possessions, knowledge, even to get more spirituality, so we will not feel our lack so acutely.

Gluttony — stuffing the void with food and drink. It is often said that "We are what we eat," but too often we eat because we do not know what or who we are.

Lust — to force a so-called union with another because we feel inwardly so disunited; to employ power over another's body to compensate for a sense of our own powerlessness

Envy — when we feel we have no fortune we will necessarily be sad at another's good fortune. When we dislike ourselves for not having

---

[9]*Meister Eckhart: Teacher and Preacher,* p. 110.

enough of whatever, we are going to dislike others who have more of whatever.

Anger — how easily we are threatened when we feel we are lacking. How intense our self-hatred is when we experience failure within. When we despise ourseives, rage is our only option.

Pride — a common saying is that pride is at the bottom of all sins. But what is at the bottom of pride? A terrifying feeling of insignificance. When we feel worthless we are driven to cloak shame with arrogance. The lower our self-esteem, the haughtier our hubris. When we feel dead, we crave acclaim to assure us we are not.

Sloth — even sloth results from a deadly feeling, a feeling of emptiness. But in sloth we desire to settle into that hole, to be comfortable in our emptiness. Sloth is to believe in, fully accept and to be content to rot in our self-made grave. But sloth is the most cunning of all sins. It can be camouflaged by frantic activity, activity designed to keep us in the tomb, rather than face our resurrection.

• • • •

These capital sins come in so many assorted flavors as to defy counting. All, however, are reduced to one: the desire for power! To compensate for feelings of weakness we frantically reach for power. Because we feel stone cold we made a Promethean attempt to steal the gods' fire.

Sins are our feeble attempts to seize an imagined divinity, in order to bolster our frail humanity. The true God is satisfied with our humanity. He made it and his Son took it for himself. By becoming flesh, the Son accepted our humanity completely, with all its supposed weaknesses and failures, including its mortality.

Even though God and his Son accept our humanity, we do not. It does not measure up to our standards. The standards are the ones we have fabricated in the likeness of "the gods." To us our humanity is too weak, totally lacking in that power our idols seem to have in abundance.

So we move against our "weak" humanity. We punish who we are. This moving against ourselves, this punishment of ourselves comprises all our sins.

Sins and punishment are connected, but the problem is we are inclined to put the label of "punisher" on the wrong person. We assume that it is God who punishes us, if not in this life, surely in the next. Theology speaks of "punishment due to sins" and there *is* punishment associated with sins, but God does not cause the punishment.

In the mid-1960s I was somewhat surprised when a priest friend Joseph Martin said very matter-of-factly: "God never has in the past, does not now, nor ever will punish anyone." At the time that sounded rather novel. I had just completed twenty-three years of education where a major theological premise was that God does indeed punish us.

In fact the spirituality of those years seemed to be centered on what to do, if not to avoid God's punishment, at least to lessen it. For only the saints avoided God's punishment altogether. The best the rest of us could hope for was a punishment that would be terrible (50,000 to 75,000 years in purgatory) but at least not eternal.

Most o-f us second graders did not know how long eternity was, but we knew it was a long time to be punished by someone as big as God. Just how this idea of God as the one who punishes sinners received such wide acceptance after the life, death and resurrection of Jesus is hard to understand. How did the God whom Jesus told us to call "Abba" (Daddy) become the One who punishes? And for eternity, no less! When and how did the father of the Prodigal Son get turned into a sadist? The two most influential Christian teachers in the western Church saw punishment as *our* doing, not God's.

Even St. Augustine who has a reputation for stressing the judgment and punishment of God admits that ultimately it is we who oppose ourselves. "He who does not love God...is not unfittingly said to hate himself since he does that which is opposed to himself and pursues himself as though he were his own enemy. This is certainly a tragic delusion...many do what is most fatal to themselves."[10]

"Opposing," "pursuing," being our "own enemy" is the punishment due to sins. This punishment is certainly a "tragic delusion" and "most fatal," but it is we who are the executioners of our pain, not God.

Eight centuries after Augustine, St. Thomas Aquinas added: "In so far as [a] sin consists in [our] turning away from God, the punishment that corresponds is the *pain of loss*."[11] Despite such authoritative voices telling us that a disordered soul is its own punishment, many Christians still insist that God punishes us. And what is even sadder, they see God punishing us in a way (with fire) and for "time" (eternity) that even the most perverse human could not inflict on a worst enemy.

God has nothing to do with punishment. As C. S. Lewis wrote, "The door to Hell is locked from the inside."[12] Unlike us, God knows we are hurting *before* we commit sins. To add more hurt or punishment *because* of sins would be absurd. In fact, it would be the beginning of further sins.

Pain and hurt call for compassion, not punishment; pity, not condemnation. Does a parent punish a child who cries at night because the child feels alone, empty and frightened? Unfortunately, sometimes earthly parents in their own intense self-hatred do; but God never does.

For God does not play by our rules. To think he does, to think it is God who punishes us, may be the worst kind of blasphemy possible, that sin against the Holy Spirit of which Christ spoke, sins against the love of God. For God sees underneath our sins and knows they are conceived in misery.

[10]St. Augustine, "The Trinity," translated by Stephen McKenna, in *The Fathers of The Church,* vol. 45 (Washington, D.C.: Catholic University of America Press), p. 436.

[11]St. Thomas Aquinas, *Summa Theologica,* vol. 19, 1st Part, Q 87, Art 4, Response to Obj.; emphasis added.

[12]C. S. Lewis, *The Joyful Christian* (New York: Macmillan Publishing Company, 1977), p. 226.

Sins are our attempt to annihilate ourselves because we feel so miserable about who we are. Why would God add more punishment to us knowing that our sins originate in a humiliating sense of shame? For God to punish would be tantamount to punishing a newborn baby for being born vulnerably naked. Could God really be such a punisher?

A Punishing God?

We have asked why the idea of a punishing God has such wide acceptance among Christians. We have mentioned the psychological reasons for this being our inclination to punish ourselves. We then project the duty of punisher onto God, who we believe will punish us, because, in our conscious or subconscious, we think we deserve punishment.

But besides this psychological reason, it cannot be denied that many places in the Bible speak of punishment. There are many examples in the Old Testament, with Deuteronomy 32:35 probably being the best known: "Vengeance is mine" (RSV). To most people the words of the psalmist express the view of punishment as presented in the Old Testament: "Sinners shall all alike be punished" (Ps 37:28).

In the light of such a tradition it is surprising just how few times punishment is mentioned in the New Testament. None of the evangelists uses the word at all, except Matthew, the most "Old Testament" Gospel.[13] And Matthew uses the word once, in a parable. His story of the Last Judgment concludes with: "and they will go off into eternal punishment" (Mt 25:46).

In all of his letters Paul likewise uses the word just once, where he speaks about "a much worse punishment" (Heb 10:29). Nevertheless, it must be recognized that despite the scarcity of New Testament references, the Bible does speak of punishment for evil behavior. Also, even if the Bible does not explicitly say so, it is implied that it is God who does the punishing. How can we square our repeated statements that God does not punish with these biblical texts?

---

[13]See "The Last Judgment" below, pp. 111–113.

The answer is in the text itself. Scripture reports a progression of revelation. The New Testament moves beyond the Old. Jesus' words, "Love your enemies and do good to those who hurt you" (Mt 5:44), move beyond "an eye for an eye, tooth for a tooth" (Dt 19:21). The Old Testament teaching that there is a "time for war" (Eccl 3:8) is not on the same moral plane as the New Testament's "Pray for your persecutors" (Mt 5:44).

To deny this moral progression is to minimize the message of Christ: "You heard it said to you that...but *I* say to you..." (Mt 5:21–43). This means that the literal meaning of much of the Old Testament is not acceptable for the people of the New. There are basic theological truths in the Old Testament, but the fuller development of their expression is not yet present. Such is the case with the connection between sins and punishment.

The tension continues in part into the New Testament. At one time Jesus said he came only for the Jews, telling his disciples: "do not visit pagan territory. Do not enter a Samaritan town. Go instead to the lost sheep of Israel" (Mt 10:5). Then he later described his mission as including the Gentiles. "I have other sheep that do not belong to this fold" (Jn 10:16). And, in fact, one person who bears witness to him is a Samaritan, the woman at the well. "Many of the Samaritans of that town began to believe in Him because of the word of the woman who testified" (Jn 4:39).

It is also true that the Scriptures were not written in a vacuum. The sacred writers were people of their time who expressed themselves in a way understandable to themselves and others. They also each selected and arranged the sayings and acts of Jesus with a view to illuminating difficulties and questions that had arisen in the early Church. God's word is not bound to one culture or one time.

Paul's understanding, for example, of the relationship of women to men was bound to his time and culture as was his view that the end of time was imminent. Each generation has the task of pruning from revelation the accessories of culture and custom.

Paul, rooted firmly in his Pharisaic tradition, still viewed God as a punishing God, although he saw that we are saved by God's mercy and our faith in him. There is a certain inconsistency in these two simultaneous views held by Paul, understandable because he was a man who had come into a newly revealed order of life after spending early adulthood in passionate belief of an earlier order.

The core of Christian revelation is that God saves, not punishes, sinners, and Paul insists on this point: "It is precisely in this that God proves His love for us: that while we were still sinners Christ died for us" (Rom 5:8). Punishment did not come "while we were still sinners"; salvation came instead. Paul here is passing on the heart of Christ's message, "I have not come to call the righteous but sinners" (Mt 9:13). The distinct revelation of the New Testament is that sins call for salvation and healing, not punishment. All of the New Testament writers held onto this revelation even though their manner of expression at times may have in effect clouded this central teaching. The gospels *do* speak of fire, of wailing and torment. This anguish is described as going on forever. It is depicted as never ending. This is so, but only if it is going on now.

Eternal punishment is a description of a present condition, our self-condemnation, which will continue as long as we engage in it. Our self-punishment will continue eternally, *if* we so choose.

Eternal punishment is self-punishment. It is *now* and it can continue if we want it to. The eternal fire, the weeping and gnashing of teeth, is what we are presently experiencing whenever we give rein to our internal dividedness.

How do we feel when our inner split causes us to judge others as being no good, bad, or as not being what they should be? We feel awful! We are gnashing our teeth at them.

How do we feel when we separate ourselves from the party, then go off and cry; we weep at our exclusiveness, our isolation, but we don't desire to come out of it. When we judge and separate others, the weeping and gnashing of teeth is already going on in us or we wouldn't have judged others to begin with. We could not have separated ourselves from other people if we were not separated within ourselves.

That inner separation is the gnashing of our teeth against ourselves, and that burns. We couldn't see others as bad and hurt them if we hadn't first seen ourselves as bad and hurt ourselves. Self-punishment! That's hell! And it can last forever. The most frightening thought about this punishment is that we are tempted to choose it.

There is the biblical truth that sins and punishment are associated. This is essential! But whereas the ancients would have attributed the punishment to God, we can see it as self-induced and self-inflicted.

The ability and willingness to accept the essence of this revelation, while interpreting the means and manner of the revelation for our times can even be applied to the expressions of Christ. Christ did not know of jet airplanes, nor did he hear of depression, schizophrenia or the death wish. He did not know epilepsy could be medically treated. He dealt with these afflictions in the terms of his time and spoke of them in the terms of his time.

This brings us to a subject prevalent at the time of Christ, and one with which he dealt — the devil. We have been discussing guilt, punishment and human destruction. Since the devil traditionally has been associated with these topics it is fitting that we speak at least briefly about this symbol of evil.

The Devil

Christ, like his contemporaries, believed in a personal being that was out to destroy humankind. He believed that Satan, or the Devil, was an actual creature. I think we can understand and accept the underlying ideas about the devil, i.e., a destructive force inimical to human wholeness, without necessarily accepting the cultural and religious trappings which surrounded the ideas at the time of Christ.

Although a complete history of the development of the notion of the devil in Judaic and Christian thought is a book in itself, we can summarize the history. The idea of a devil was not present in the beginnings of the Old Testament traditions. The appearance and then growth of the idea has as good a summary as I have seen in an article published in 1982 by Kenneth Woodward and David Gater of *Newsweek* magazine. They quote the prominent Mircea Eliade of the University of Chicago Divinity School: "The figure of Satan probably developed under the influence of Iranian dualism"; and George MacRae, a Jesuit of the Harvard Divinity School: "The Old Testament simply does not contain a personal Devil who is the principle of evil and God's adversary."

From these two and other sources Woodward and Gater conclude: "In the last four centuries before Christ the Israelites gradually developed a need for a powerful Devil. That need was born out of the spiritual despair arising from their dashed nationalistic hopes...a new theology was needed to explain their persistent misfortunes." The Israelites came up with the idea of the devil as a countervailing force to God, drawing on obscure scriptures written in the centuries immediately before and after Christ.

Written mostly by apocalyptic Jews and early Christians, these writings fashioned a devil in the image of the Persian "Ahriman," the prince of darkness, linking the devil with the serpent of Eden as the cause of human mortality. Many rabbis shunned these ideas because they could turn the Judaic faith into dualism, with two equal Gods.

The ideas fit the Christians' picture, though. The devil was a superb foil to highlight Christ's role: light vs. dark, truth vs. falsehood, life vs. death. The early Christians thus emphasized that Christ cast out demons. But the devil and his legion, the "powers and principalities" named by Paul (Eph 6:12), are not equals of God but rather are lesser creatures.

Woodward and Gater conclude: "The real religious lesson woven into the long history of the devil is that ultimately only God can divest man from his drive toward self-destruction…a trivial personification is hardly adequate to symbolize the mystery of evil that even non-believers must confront."[14]

We need to hold onto the essence of the devil and its self-destructiveness in order to see its role in the life of humankind. It is not necessary, although it is possible, to view the devil as personified in the myths of other ancient religions. And it is essential, to avoid a dualistic instead of a monotheistic religion, to avoid equating any devil symbol as equal with God; all creations are creations of God, subject to God; and every being, in order to have existence, must be grounded in the Supreme Being, God!

Christ knew better than anyone that there is a force of darkness and death that oppresses humankind. For the purposes of this book, we need only have a minimum idea of a mystery in life that destroys the human being.

Thomas Merton, in speaking to his religious community at Gethsemani Abbey, seldom spoke of the devil. On one of the rare occasions that he did, he seemed to have a very balanced approach. He held to the essence of the teaching about the devil and let go of the accidents:

---

[14]"Giving the Devil His Due," *Newsweek,* August 30, 1982, pp. 72–74.

I don't know what this force is, a personal force, or however you want to look at it... Even if they prove that "it" is a projection of something in me, that doesn't make any difference. "It" can still wreck me.[15]

The theme in this point of view of the devil is balance. Too much attention to the devil unbalances us if we neglect to heal the interior divisions we may have. There is danger in using the devil as an excuse when the appropriate diagnosis is interior matters that we can attend.

Also, to preoccupy oneself with a personal devil gives it power over us, and over people who care about us or who associate with us. It is like the child who believes in a bogeyman in the basement. The child's fear has some control over the child. He needs a night light. And the child causes the father to lock the basement door, so the child feels safer. The child's fear has some effect on others, as well as himself.

At the Easter Vigil liturgy we renounce "Satan and all his works." It is important to recognize the practicality of our words. This means we acknowledge that we are indeed tempted toward "non-existence and self-destruction," to use Dostoevsky's astute description of the devil.[16]

For aren't our ego thoughts, those thoughts of being as we "should be" where we are always the greatest, the best, aren't such hero thoughts our trip into non-existence? And isn't the fact that we refuse to accept ourselves, that we are often hard on ourselves, isn't that engaging in self-destruction?

To renounce "Satan and all his works," besides the obvious meaning, could also be seen as a renunciation of these tendencies as they manifest themselves in our thoughts and actions, and nothing is more efficacious than this renunciation to ward off a devil, any kind of a devil, personal or otherwise. For to refuse the allure of non-existence and self-destruction, that adversary that can "wreck me," is to enlighten with grace the fact of original sin.

---

[15]From Merton's Talks to Monks, Tape #147.
[16]Dostoevsky, *The Brothers Karamazof*, p. 130.

Part Four

Original Sin and Nakedness

Original sin is an illusion. We see it because we have created it; it's real because we have made it real. Our illusion of alienation from God is real to us but not to God. We believe we are separated from God, that we are bad. God doesn't believe our myths. In this sense we know more than God! God knows only good; we know both the good *and* the bad.

When Adam told God that he was afraid and hid because he was naked, God asked him "Who told you that you were naked?" (Gn 3:11), or in other words "who told you that you were bad?" It is a rhetorical question for God himself answers it immediately. "You have eaten from the tree of which I had forbidden you to eat!" (Gn 3:11). In other words: "Adam, you know that you are naked because you have chosen to know both the good *and* the bad. And in looking at yourself, you have judged yourself to be bad; you have judged yourself to be guilty, thinking that you are not what you should be."

"Who told you that you were naked?" The most fundamental question ever put to humankind and the answer is: "Adam (that is, humanity), you tell yourself that you are naked, that you are bad. You judge that you're guilty."

After Adam and Eve had eaten the fruit: "Then the eyes of both of them were opened and they realized [judged] that they were naked..." (Gn 3:7). God did not say to Adam that he was naked, that he was bad or that Adam was guilty. God did not make those judgments against Adam. Adam said this about himself. He judged himself and this judgment against himself was the result of eating of the tree of good *and* bad.

Once we humans choose to be "like the gods," by necessity we are going to judge ourselves as not what we "should be," as *not* being "like the gods." Once we set up that false standard, by necessity we are going to have to see ourselves as naked, as bad. We are going to have to see ourselves as guilty!

Adam made "the bad" (his illusion) real. Adam made his "guilt" real, but to himself, not to God. God didn't know Adam was naked or bad; Adam had to tell him. He had to tell him about his illusion of guilt. Adam had to tell God something God did not know.

Yes, we humans "know" more than God. We know that we are naked, that we are bad, that we are guilty of evil, just because we are human beings. The catch is that this "evil" we know, this "guilt" we know, is an illusion. We know more than God in the sense that we know our illusion. We know what isn't.

God has no dealings with our illusions, our original "guilt," our original "sin" except to save us from it. God saves us from our illusion of guilt, our illusion of being bad, by his light. God's light reveals to us the goodness of creation, reveals to us our true identity as God's children. God's light is his Son, Jesus Christ.

In Jesus Christ, God reveals that we are each his "beloved Son" (Mt 3:17). God can see only a reflection of himself and so everyone God sees is his Son or Daughter. The only person God sees is his reflected Word, Jesus Christ.

When God looks at us he sees Jesus, and only Jesus, the innocent, guiltless Jesus. St. Augustine expresses this by saying that heaven (the kingdom of God) consists in "one Christ loving Himself."[1] The kingdom of God consists in my true self (Christ) loving another's true self (Christ). Or, the kingdom of God is the reality of Christ (who I am) loving Christ (who is also every other person): "one Christ loving Himself" in St. Augustine's words. And this kingdom of God (heaven) is

---

[1]St. Augustine, "Sermon to the People," in Emile Mersch, S.J., *The Whole Church* (Milwaukee, Wisconsin: Bruce Publishing Company, 1938), p. 347.

now. It's in the midst of us. And it is all God sees because it is the only reality there is, the only "Idea," or "Word" in God's mind.

Even now God does not see our nakedness. Unlike us, God is unaware of the good and the bad. God notices only the good in creation. In every person God knows only his created Word, Jesus.[2]

---

[2]The idea that God sees only his Son Jesus is discussed more completely in "Our True Self" below, pp. 118–122.

Sins and Self-Forgiveness

That God sees only the good of creation, sees only his Son Jesus in every human being holds true not only in our original state of creation but also when we lose that state and commit sins. God sees us as his Son not only in our original innocence but when we forgo or abandon that innocence and trespass. When we act out of our false self and commit sins, God doesn't alter his view of us.

But if it be true that God's view of us is not influenced by our sins and trespasses, why do we ask God to forgive us? Why do we pray "Forgive us our trespasses" if God doesn't take notice of our trespasses? Because *we* take notice of our trespasses; *we* are influenced by our sinful acts and we need to forgive *ourselves.*

In asking God to forgive us our sins, we are asking God for the grace to forgive ourselves, to look upon ourselves as God does, non-judgmentally and compassionately. As soon as we are aware of sins we must forgive ourselves, and for this we need God's grace and light. The longer we delay and dwell negatively on the fact that we have sinned, the guiltier we will feel. The longer we remain in the darkness of guilt the more the light is obscured. Through the grace of God we must let the sins go, we must forgive ourselves, otherwise our feelings of guilt will grow.

We have spoken about our primordial or original sense of guilt. This is the illusory guilt that leads us to believe that we are separated from God, that we are bad, wrong, guilty, that we are naked. It is this self-alienation that leads us to try to be like "the gods," i.e., like we "should be."

Our effort to live up to our idols is, in effect, a moving against ourselves, a self-punishment. When we act out this self-punishment we commit sins.

So our actual sins are the result of our primordial sense of guilt which means we feel guilty *before* we commit a sin, that there is a sense of guilt *prior* to any guilty act. And it is this prior sense of guilt that causes us to commit sins. Freud spoke of "the obscure sense of guilt *before* the deed": "Paradoxical as it may sound, I must maintain that the sense of guilt was present *prior* to the transgression."[3]

To illustrate this point there is the example of the adolescent who feels he has failed at everything from school work to acquiring friends. He feels totally worthless and powerless to change his lot. To compensate for his guilty feelings he vandalizes his school, a tangible symbol of his failure.

Or there is the adult who feels he is not a successful human being because he is financially unsuccessful. He compensates for his supposed guilt by embezzling funds. We see the vandalism and embezzling, the guilty deeds, but what we often fail to see is that these people are laboring under a double sense of guilt.

The obvious guilt is the guilt for their transgression. The obscure guilt is that which was theirs from their feelings of inferiority. And it is this illusory guilt which leads to transgressions. This guilt is the cause of all our actual sins. We commit sins because we feel guilty! Then our actual sins make us feel even more guilty.

Hopefully it is now obvious why we cannot allow the guilt when it arises from our sins, our real guilt, to grow. For this sense of guilt for our actual sins will reinforce our original guilt.

Our real guilt intensifies our illusory guilt because our real guilt convinces us that we are surely not what we "should be," the proof being that we did this sinful deed. Now we are more convinced than ever that we are bad or wrong. The guilt for our sins has strengthened our primordial sense of guilt which itself is the cause of our sins.

---

[3]Sigmund Freud, *Character and Culture* (New York: Crowell-Collier, 1963), p. 179.

Unless we let go of our real guilt we will be caught in a vicious circle. We will feel guilty for our sins which heightens our original or primordial guilt which in turn causes us to sin again, and the cycle repeats itself. Our sins begin in guilt, end in guilt, and then start over.

To break this downward spiral we must forgive ourselves immediately. This self-forgiveness is difficult. As we previously mentioned there are reasons we have for holding onto guilt. Our guilt ties us to our security figures and is therefore itself a source of security. We *like* to feel guilty, so much so that we need the grace of God in order to let go of guilt. We need God to free us from "the gods," those to whom we are bound by guilt.

God, unlike "the gods" whom we create, is a source of our freedom and so is not involved in our cycle of guilt. God can't enter into our illusory world of separation but he can and does love us. It is only by God's light and love that we can break out of our guilt/sin/guilt/spiral.

We see sins in ourselves and others. God sees only the anguish and fear that leads to these sins. Because of Christ, God sees us all as innocent, in pain but innocent! His love heals that pain for it is that pain which causes us to sin.

Pain is looked upon with compassion, not judgment. Pain calls forth God's mercy, not his condemnation.

We need to ask God to "Forgive us our trespasses" realizing while we do that it is we who, through God's grace and light, are forgiving ourselves. God's compassion deals with forgiveness only indirectly, through others and ourselves.

Through the sacramental system the church has always taught that forgiveness is effected through people. We need people (the church) to confirm our forgiveness. But what we have failed to sufficiently realize is that the most important person in our forgiveness is ourselves. Unless we forgive ourselves, the church can't. "…[W]hatever you declare bound on earth shall be held bound in heaven…" (Mt 18:18).

If we choose not to forgive ourselves and to bind ourselves to our world of guilt and fear we are denying God's world of grace and light. We are binding God. For although God does not *directly* forgive us our sins, he does give us the grace to forgive ourselves.

Since we have separated ourselves from ourselves, our forgiveness is necessary. Since God has not separated himself from us, his forgiveness is unnecessary. God can't forgive us, for he has never judged us as guilty. "Our Lord God cannot...forgive, because he cannot be angry."[4] He has never judged us as guilty because all God sees is his Son, his Son in us. There is no one God can judge. There is in every person only his Son, who is innocent. "Our Father may not, and does not wish to assign more blame to us than to His own beloved Son Jesus."[5] "I saw God assigned to us no kind of blame."[6]

A woman once related to me an experience that verified in a grace-filled way the truth of these statements by Julian of Norwich — that God does not assign blame to us. At a time in her life when she was feeling the oppressive weight of her sinfulness, this woman turned in prayer to God. In her prayer, she had the courage to ask for the grace to see herself as she really was.

Even though she felt miserable she wanted to know the truth about herself; she wanted to see herself as God sees her. In the chapel a crucifix hung on the wall and as she prayed the woman's attention was drawn to that crucifix. Right at that time a verse from Scripture flashed across her mind: "And they saw only Jesus."

These words are from the episode of the Transfiguration, where Peter, James and John saw Jesus transfigured and standing with Moses and Elijah. The episode concludes: "a bright cloud cast a shadow over them, then from the cloud came a voice that said, 'This is My beloved Son with Whom I am well pleased...' When the disciples heard this, they fell prostrate and were very much afraid. But Jesus came and touched them, saying, 'Rise and do not be afraid.' And when the disciples raised their eyes, they saw no one else but Jesus alone" (Mt 17:5–8).

---

[4]*Julian of Norwich, "Showings,"* p. 263.
[5]Ibid., p. 275.
[6]Ibid., p. 257.

The interpretation of her experience seems clear. She had asked that it be revealed how God sees her. Then the words struck her "and they saw only Jesus." Just as in the Scriptural account the disciples see only Jesus, so likewise God sees only Jesus.

Here was a person who was almost overwhelmed with a sense of her sinfulness. Naturally she would expect that God also would be seeing her sinfulness and accordingly look upon her as blameworthy. But her expectation and sense of blame proved groundless as she realized God "cannot be angry." Even though at the time she was seeing only her sinfulness, it was made clear to her that as God looks at her God sees only Jesus, the blameless Jesus. Accordingly she took to herself Jesus' words to his disciples, "Do not be afraid." Her internal turmoil was replaced with calm and peace; her shame and fear by trust and love. She "knew," that is, she understood with her whole being, that "Our Father may not, and does not wish to, assign more blame to us than to His own beloved Son, Jesus." And she became aware that the words the Father spoke to Jesus are intended for her and indeed for us all: "This is my beloved Son in Whom I am well pleased."

How can God assign blame to his beloved Son? How could God condemn and judge one in whom God is well pleased? Of course he cannot and does not condemn and judge such a person. Of course God cannot judge and condemn us.

Christic Doesn't Judge

"The Father judges no one…" Then Jesus continues: "but has assigned all judgment to the Son" (Jn 5:22). What does "…and has assigned all judgment to the Son" mean? At first it sounds as if even though the Father doesn't judge, the Son does.

But to say all judgment has been given to the Son has a much more significant meaning. To say that all judgment has been given to the Son is to say, in effect, that the Son became a human being.

Earlier in his gospel, St. John expressed this by saying, "the word became flesh and made his dwelling among us…" (Jn 1:14). To become flesh, to become a man means to have the capacity to judge, the capacity to condemn. By becoming a man, the Son of God entered into the human world of judgment.

As Spirit, the Son of God could not judge or condemn for a Spirit has no internal division, no parts and therefore is incapable of judging. To say that the Son has been given all judgment merely highlights the truth that all humans are able to judge and that the Son became a human being.

To be a human being means to be able to make judgments. Divinity is incapable of making judgments because God can't separate or cut himself off from anyone or anything.

As God, the Son could not judge, but as the man, Jesus, the Son could judge. He could separate himself from others. "The Father has given over to [Jesus] power to pass judgment because he is Son of Man…" (Jn 5:27). *Because* the Son became a human being (the Son of Man) judgment was possible for him.

But did Christ follow this human characteristic to judge? Did he act as we do and divide, separate and condemn? To be given the power to judge is one thing. To use that power is something else. A person can have the ability to do something yet refrain from doing it.

As a man, the Son had the power to judge. But did he use that power? No, Jesus did not judge! Immediately after saying that all judgment has been given to the Son, Jesus continued: "the man who hears my word and has faith in him who sent me possesses eternal life. He does not come under condemnation [judgment]" (Jn 5:24). Then he explicitly said that the Son of Man came into the world not to judge the world but that the world might be saved through him: "I do not condemn [judge]....I did not come to condemn the world but to save the world" (Jn 12:47). "I do not judge anyone" (Jn 8:15).

How can we so readily put the title of judge on one who so obviously denied the role of judge? How can we assume that the one who said "I came that they might have life and have it to the full" (Jn 10:10) is going to separate himself from us, is going to condemn us?

Doesn't it seem strange that so many Christians insist on seeing Christ as the one who will judge or condemn them, whereas he saw himself solely in terms of life? "I am the...life" (Jn 14:6). Life excludes separation, judgment and condemnation. As St. Paul said "there is no condemnation [judgment] for those who are in Christ Jesus" (Rom 8:1). If there is no judgment for those who are in Christ, how can Christ be called a judge?

By telling us that all judgment has been given to him but that he was not a judge, Jesus was saying that by becoming a man he has entered our world of judgment and condemnation, but that he doesn't partake of our mentality. He is among us, but not of our divided mind for he has come from the Father and his unity.

Although the Son did enter our world of judgment, he disassociated himself from our split way of thinking, from our propensity to separate, divide and judge. As he said, "You are of this world. I am not of this world" (Jn 8:23 RSV). That is, "You eat of the tree of good *and* evil; I eat only of the tree of life." Jesus dwelt among us but would not take part in our dualistic world that demands judgments.

Our world needs judges. We can't imagine a world devoid of judging. Maybe this is why we too readily see Jesus our Savior as Jesus our judge. We need a judge to keep our world together. On one occasion a man approached Christ and said "Teacher, tell my brother to give me my share of our inheritance," and Jesus replied, "Friend, who has set me up as your judge or arbiter?" (Lk 12:14). Jesus refused the role of judge. He refused to be drawn into our illusory world of division.

In our world we divide and judge, but Jesus was coming from a different perspective. Although being in our world of judgment he was preaching God's world of non-judgment. He was preaching the kingdom of God. In the kingdom of God judgment is impossible. How can you judge or divide an inheritance that belongs to everyone equally?

No one in the kingdom can say to Jesus, "Tell my brother to divide the inheritance with me." As soon as we say "divide," "separate," as soon as we say "judge," we have removed ourselves from the kingdom. Judgment and the kingdom of God are in opposition, for "the Father...judges no one" (Jn 5:22).

And the Son judges no one! Even though as a man he has the capacity to judge, he does, in fact, judge no one.

And the Holy Spirit, the unity between the Father and the Son, can judge no one. The principle of love cannot divide or separate. The source of unity can't be divisive.

"Who [or what] will separate us from the love of Christ?" (Rom 8:35). "I am certain that neither death nor life, neither angels nor principalities, neither the present, nor the future, nor powers, neither height nor depth nor any other creature, will be able to separate us [judge us] from the love of God that comes to us in Jesus, our Lord" (Rom 8:38–39).

There can be no division in God and there can be no division in God's kingdom. There can be no judgment in either. Our divided minds can't even begin to comprehend a non-judgmental existence, one of complete simplicity. The very idea threatens us because it shatters our world.

For our sense of security we have to see ourselves as continually judging, continually dividing into good and bad and we naturally project our mental workings onto God. It is difficult for us to realize that the divine mind is not like our human mind. The human mind (the result of eating of the tree of good *and* evil) is split. The divine mind (symbolized by the tree of life) has no such split. God's mind is whole.

The Last Judgment

In one of the gospels there is the story that we call "The Last Judgment." In the story we automatically assume that Christ is to be the judge, the cause of punishment. But is Christ the judge, the one who is doing the dividing and separation or is he the revealer, the one showing us the results of *our* separating and dividing, the effects of our judging? If punishment is inflicted, who is inflicting it, Christ or ourselves?

Before we look at this passage it may be well to note that the account of the last judgment is recorded only in the gospel of Matthew. This is the gospel written especially for Jews who were steeped in the notion of God as judge.

Matthew is the most Old Testament of all the gospels, and we would expect to find a heavy emphasis on judgment and punishment. It is Matthew who repeatedly uses the phrase "weeping and gnashing of teeth" which is used nowhere else in the New Testament except once in Luke. In a similar vein, Matthew uses the word "hell" about a dozen times, Mark and Luke three times each, and John and Paul, who comprise the largest part of the New Testament, never mention it.

Matthew's story of the last judgment begins with Jesus saying that he will separate the sheep from the goats. The basis for this separation, this division, this judgment will be how we relate to people, especially to the stranger, those in prison, the hungry, the naked, the thirsty, those whom Jesus calls "these least ones" (Mt 25:45). These are the people that society tends to cut off, to separate, that is, to judge. These are the people that we judge, that we cut off from our company.

In telling us this story, Christ is telling us that the last judgment concerns how we relate to people whom we exclude from our company.

He reminds us that it is we who separate ourselves from people when we don't see ourselves as one with them. Our judgment is tied up with this kind of person, those we don't like, people we call "them" instead of "us." The "least ones" are the "them" in our life.

The last judgment concerns those people about whom we have made a judgment — "they are not like they should be!" That is the point of the story: *we* have made a judgment. We do not want to associate with those we don't like. *We* have excluded them, separated them, divided and cut them off.

It is *we* who have separated humankind. We, not Christ, have separated into sheep and goats, those we think are as they "should be," and those we think are not as they "should be." Not Christ, but we, have made those judgments and those judgments have far-reaching ramifications.

There are results which occur from our dividing humankind. Our judging has effects on others and ourselves. Not only does our judging affect others, it is also an indication of what is going on inside us. By judging others as undesirable we are judging ourselves as undesirable.

Others are merely reflections of how we are judging ourselves, for not being as we "should be." When we condemn others as bad we are merely externalizing our self-condemnation. We are saying that we are bad! When we separate or exclude others we are merely acting out our inner separation, our inner split by which we exclude part of ourselves, the part we think "should not be," the part that is not like "the gods."

When we judge others we are acting out of our inner dualism which judges and divides us into good and bad. We then project our inner separation onto the world and separate others into good or bad, into the sheep and the goats.

If we are confirmed in our desire to hold onto our split self, if we are confirmed in our decision to condemn ourselves as reflected in others, if we are determined to continually divide ourselves, if we say "this will be our last judgment," then it will be!

We have chosen our last judgment. We have rejected our true self. We have divided ourselves. We have chosen inner alienation instead of inner wholeness, and Christ won't, and indeed can't, overrule our choice.

The story of the last judgment is not about Christ making judgments against us but about how we make judgments against ourselves. It is a story about how we then project our self-judgment onto others and divide and separate ourselves from them in the same way that we are divided and separated within ourselves. It is true that "those who have done wicked deeds will come to the resurrection of condemnation [judgment]" (Jn 5:29).

But we are making that judgment, not Christ. We have determined our last judgment. As Matthew's parable says: "When the Son of Man comes in His glory… He will say on those of His left hand [the goats] 'go away from me, with *your* curse upon you, to eternal fire' " (Mt 25:31–41 JB). The only curse put upon us is the curse we put upon ourselves.

The Rich Man and Lazarus

Christ told the parable of the rich man and the poor man, Lazarus (Lk 16:19–31), which makes the same point as did the parable of the last judgment. The rich man excluded Lazarus. He separated and divided himself from the poor man: he judged him.

After the rich man died he was in a place of torment and begged Abraham to send Lazarus to cool his tongue with water. Abraham replied that this was impossible because a "great chasm," a "great divide," existed between the rich man and Lazarus.

Yes, there was a great divide between the two. There was a separation. They had been cut off from one another.

But who made the cut, who made that judgment that separated them? Not Abraham, but the rich man had made that judgment. He has judged Lazarus. He had separated himself and now he is experiencing the effects of his division, the effects of his judgment. Now in a place of fire the rich man asks that his tongue be cooled.

It is the tongue that we use to pass judgment: "They are bad, he isn't what he should be, she is wrong." The tongue is the instrument we use to divide the sheep from the goats. The rich man had passed judgment, had made this division at his table. He had eaten sumptuously, not even sharing the crumbs with Lazarus. The table, the special place of fellowship, is where separation and judgment took place.

In this parable, like the story of separating the sheep from the goats, we see that it is we who do the separating. We do the judging, not God or Christ.

The last judgment is merely the outcome of how we have judged during our lives. The last judgment is present now, for the rich man was in torment while he sat at his table. It was there that he had passed judgment knowingly on another, unknowingly on himself. The rich man was in torment before he died. His tongue was on fire in this life.

In this life he passed judgment. In the afterlife he was experiencing the long-term effects of his divisive mentality. His death merely cemented his previous division.

Christic the Light

Christ is the revealer, not the judge. He reveals to us that we have judged, divided and separated. For us to say that Christ judges and condemns us is analogous to the student who says that "the teacher failed me." The teacher doesn't fail the student; the teacher merely reveals what the student has or has not done.

It is the student who fails the student; that is the reality. The teacher reveals that reality, reveals the student's work.

This is why Christ is called the Light, "the Light of the World" (Jn 9:5), because he reveals our works; he reveals what is. A light doesn't determine what is; it doesn't make the condition. It illuminates what is real and brings into focus the condition.

Christ said, "I cannot do anything of myself. I judge as I hear…" (Jn 5:30). And he also speaks, "the word itself which I have spoken will be [the] judge on the last day" (Jn 12:48 JB). Christ transmits or speaks the life of God — reality — "what He hears" to us, but he does not pass judgment. Rather he enables us to see reality, to see what is, which may unfortunately include the fact that we do judge. So Christ could say "My judgment is honest" (Jn 5:30), because he reveals the truth about our judging; he reveals the truth about ourselves.

When we say in the creed that Christ will come "to judge the living and the dead" this judgment is not what we understand by the word "to judge." To judge as Christ is not to separate and divide but to cover all with God's light and love which illuminates what we have chosen. "And this is judgment, that the light [Christ] has come into the world and people loved darkness rather than light" (Jn 3:19 RSV). The light does not judge. Judgment is that "people loved the darkness rather than the

114

light." People make the judgment. What we refer to as God's judgment is really God's revelation, God revealing to us what we have done.

In God's love we will see the effects of preferring darkness over light. Through the light of Christ we will see our deeds, see what we have done to ourselves and others by our judging.

We can accuse ourselves, but Christ can do no more than put his light and love on us. As he said, "Do not think that I will accuse you before the Father..." (Jn 5:45). One of the main theological reasons why Christ cannot accuse, judge or punish is his union with the Father.

Being equal to the Father who judges no one, Christ in his divinity can judge no one. And in his humanity Christ doesn't judge.

Condemnation or judgment is not part of Christ's message because it is not part of Christ. He didn't condemn himself, so he was incapable of condemning others. Christ's lack of condemnation, his lack of judgment, is what distinguished the New Testament from the Old.

Two contrasting stories that we join in our liturgy illustrate this distinction. The Old Testament story of Suzanna (Dn 13) has judgment and condemnation throughout, even to the end where the Elders are condemned. Judgment ends in death. The New Testament counterpart, the woman taken in adultery (Jn 8:3–11), ends with no condemnation from anyone: not the crowd, not Jesus, not even the woman herself.

In telling the woman "do not sin anymore" (Jn 8:11), Jesus is telling her "go and do not condemn yourself, do not move against yourself, do not judge yourself." To do so would only lead to further sins. For all judgment and condemnation lead to sins and death, while non-judgment and acceptance lead to life.

Our True Self

> When a man goes out of himself to find God
> he is wrong. I do not find God outside myself
> nor conceive him excepting as my own and in me.[7]
> Meister Eckhart

In Christ we come to the realization of who we are, children of God. In Christ we receive our true identity so that the Father can say to us as he said to Christ, "This is my beloved Son. My favor rests on Him" (Mt 3:17). Our true identity, our true *self*, is Christ and therefore divine. The saints had no doubts about this. "My me is God. Nor do I know myself except in God" (St. Catherine of Genoa).[8] "God is born that we may be taken up into God...man is enabled to become God..." (St. Hilary).[9] "God became man that man might become God" (St. Athanasius).[10]

These are not merely pious exaggerations of a bygone religious age. Thomas Merton used similar language. Like Meister Eckhart, Merton insisted that since God is present with us as the ground of our being, we can't experience a separation or distance between ourselves and God. "If I

---

[7]*Meister Eckhart: The Essential Sermons, Commentaries, Treatises, and Defense,* translated by Edmund Colledge and Bernard McGinn, Classics of Western Spirituality (New York: Paulist, 1981), p. 188; my paraphrase.

[8]St. Catherine of Genoa, *Vita e Dottrina,* as quoted in Evelyn Underhill, *Mysticism* (New York: E. P. Dutton, 1961), pp. 129 and 396.

[9]St. Hilary, *De Trinitate*, as quoted in Mersch, *The Whole Christ,* p. 278.

[10]St. Athanasius, *The Incarnation of the Word of God,* in *Nicene and Post-Nicene Fathers,* vol. 6 (Grand Rapids: William B. Eerdmans Publishing Co., 1957), p. 65.

find God I will find myself and if I find my true Self I will find God."[11] "There is a union of God's Spirit and our innermost [true] Self, so that we and God are in all truth one Spirit."[12]

What St. Paul called our "inner self" (Rom 7:22), Merton called our "true self." The Holy Spirit is intimately united to our true self and this makes our "true I" the "I" of Christ. He speaks about the "*humble* joy" which belongs to the Christian who realizes that "I and the Lord [Christ] are one."[13]

Since Christ is who we truly are, there is no division within us. There is Christ alone. St. Augustine, in his teaching on the mystical body of Christ, identifies Christ with us in the boldest possible language. "If we consider ourselves…we shall see that He [Christ] *is* ourselves." He then puts the following words on the lips of Christ: "In Me they too are Myself…truly are me."[14]

This total identity of Christ with humanity, our divinization, is most clearly taught by the Eastern Church Fathers although the West also made its contribution to the doctrine. The Fathers see the Incarnation — the Son of God becoming a human being — as continuing through history. They see humanity prolonging or extending the Incarnation, so that the particular Incarnation (Jesus Christ) continues and becomes the "collective Incarnation" (all humanity). "The Word became flesh and made His dwelling among us" (Jn 1:14). This "Infleshing of God" continues in us. "God's only begotten Word [Christ] is always with the human race, united to and mingles with His own creation" (St. Irenaeus).[15]

---

[11]Thomas Merton, *New Seeds of Contemplation* (New York: New Directions, 1961), p. 36.

[12]From Merton's Talks to Monks, Tape #186.

[13]Thomas Merton, *The Inner Experience,* edited by Patrick Hart (Trappist, KY: Cistercian Studies, 1983–1984), p. 8.

[14]St. Augustine, "Sermon to the People," as quoted in Mersch, *The Whole Christ,* p. 432.

[15]St. Irenaeus, *Against Heresies,* in *The Ante-Nicene Fathers,* vol. 1 (Grand Rapids: William B. Eerdmans Publishing Co., 1977), p. 442.

The result of the union between the historical Christ and Christ now living in us, traditionally referred to as the Divine Indwelling, is what Augustine termed "the Whole Christ." "The Children of God are the body of the only Son of God, and since He is the head and we are the members there is but *one* Son of God."[16] This collective "One Son of God," this union, is "the Whole Christ." Christ himself prayed for this union, his oneness with his members: "[Father,] that they may be one as We are one, I *in them* and You in Me" and "that love with which You loved Me may be *in them* and I *in them*" (Jn 17:22, 26).

Everything that is and everyone who is is in God's kingdom, is in God's world, is in God and his love. Again St. Augustine stresses this universal love of God for everything and everyone. "God hates none of the things He has made...the love wherewith the Father loves His Son is also *in us*. God Who loves His Son cannot do otherwise than love the members of His Son...the Son is loved wholly head *and* body."[17] Nothing could exist if it were not in God's love. God's love is present in every situation and in every person, so we don't and can't merit God's love.

A popular misunderstanding of merit presupposes that God's love can be gained by what we do, so merit divides everything into meritorious or unmeritorious, worthy of God's love or unworthy of God's love. And that, besides being blasphemous is just laughable. "In the true Christian version of God's love the idea of worthiness loses its significance...the mercy of God makes the whole problem of worthiness laughable: the discovery that worthiness is of no special consequence is a true Liberation."[18]

Christ revealed God's kingdom as available to all. Some are not more worthy to receive it than others. The kingdom is open to all who are willing to receive it as a gift and allow others to receive it as a gift.

---

[16]St. Augustine, "Sermon to the People," as quoted in Mersch, *The Whole Christ,* p. 437.

[17]Ibid., p. 435; emphasis added.

[18]Merton, *New Seeds of Contemplation,* p. 75.

The kingdom of God (heaven) is not given to us as a reward for what we have done. Indeed everyone is already in the kingdom.

St. Paul speaks about the end time when "...God may be all in all" (I Cor 15:28). That "end time" can be now for us if we but open our eyes to see it. The reason we don't see God's presence now is because there is a part of us that does not want to believe in the all-inclusiveness of God's kingdom. We don't want to believe in God's universal compassion, in God's unconditional love. We want to make a judgment saying that some are worthy of this compassion and love and some are not.

God is presently showering *everyone* with mercy upon mercy. That is very threatening to us and our world. There is a part of us that doesn't like the kingdom of God. It threatens our security. That God loves *all* the people *all* the time "blows apart" our neat world of right and wrong, should be and should not be, worthy and unworthy. God's love shatters us and our world of reward and punishment, and we don't like that.

We don't like the kingdom of God — until we accept that we are included in those whom God is loving all the time. When we accept that we too are being showered with mercy upon mercy then we can allow others to be so showered. We can allow the kingdom of God to come, or rather, we can accept that it is already here. For Christ said: "I confer a Kingdom on you" (Lk 22:29), and "your Father is pleased to give you the Kingdom" (Lk 12:32), in fact Jesus already "has made us into a Kingdom" (Rv 1:6).

The acceptance of this kingdom of being totally and unconditionally loved does indeed make absurd our world of judgment, make laughable our ideal of worthiness. What a freedom to be delivered from our world of self-punishment. What a liberation to know we don't have to be ashamed of our nakedness.

"Who told you that you were naked?" Who told us? We told ourselves. We told ourselves that we are bad, that we are guilty, that we are not what we "should be." We told ourselves those destructive messages because we were ashamed that we were "just" human beings and not "like the gods."

But in Christ, who became like us, who became a human being, we don't have to believe our illusions of guilt anymore. That is good news; to know we don't have to be ashamed because we are "just" human. We don't have to hide from our humanness.

Our nakedness is not something we need to feel guilty about, but something we can rejoice in. Our supposed vulnerability, our true self, is not something we have to clothe. Rather it is Someone (Christ) whom we can love, and in so doing, also love God. For "He who knows how to love himself [his true self] loves God."[19]

---

[19]St. Augustine, "The Trinity," *The Fathers of the Church,* 45:435.

Part Five

Our False Self

If it is correct to say that we *are* our true self (our Christ-centered self) it is equally correct to say that we have a false self.

In the last chapter we spoke about our true self — that self permanently united to God. Now we must consider our false self and the need we have to be saved from its enslavement.

Our false self is that self that we create because we imagine we are separated from God. The result of having a false self is our desire (concupiscence) to be "like the gods," that is, like we "should be."

Merton described this false self as "the exterior 'I' which has a compulsive need to measure up to greatness and infallibility."[1] "This 'I' seeks recognition, applause, wants accomplishments, and success."[2] "It is the self which wants to exist outside of the reach of God's will and God's love, or outside of reality and outside of life. Such a self cannot help but be an illusion."[3]

Our false self is an illusion, but we really have the illusion. It isn't, but this "isn't" is!

"Our false self doesn't exist, it isn't there."[4] "It's alienated from our true self and therefore from God."[5] "It is the 'I' I want to exist outside of reality, therefore not known by God."[6]

---

[1]Merton, *The Inner Experience,* p. 9.

[2]Ibid., p. 4.

[3]Merton, *New Seeds of Contemplation,* p. 34.

[4]From Merton's Talks to Monks, Tape #44.

[5]Merton, *The Inner Experience,* p. 16.

[6]Merton, *New Seeds of Contemplation,* p. 34.

Since our false self has no real existence, God does not know it. He does not enter into our fiction but we have created this illusion and so become entrapped in it. An analogous situation would be the case of a child, who, trying to shut out his parents, closes his eyes. Not seeing his parents, the child believe he is separated from them. He believes his own fiction. The illusion of separation the child has created becomes real to him.

With his eyes closed, he has created a "distance" between himself and his parents, believing that since he can't see them, they can't see him. To the parents, of course, this is no separation. The parent is continually present to the child, watching and loving him.

Or, putting it another way, our illusion of separation from God is like dreaming we have committed horrible crimes. What we dreamed is not real, but we really had the dream. If we believed the bad dream and act on it, it will have negative effects on our lives for we will try to compensate for our fictional crimes.

Our false self compensates for its fictional separation by desiring the power of "the gods." It wants to be its own source of life, to be omnipotent. Our word "power" comes from the Latin *posse* which means "to be able" or simply, "to be." Merton says that "original sin is related to our instinct *to be.*"[7] In effect, he is saying that original sin is related to our instinct for *power.* This striving for power leads us to sins, which in turn, increases our sense of alienation from ourselves, others and God.

How can our self-imposed alienation be healed and our real guilt — that is, guilt for what we have done, not for who we are — be forgiven? How can we be reconciled with our true self and with God? How can we be saved from our sins?

The first thing that has to be done is to admit that we do have a false self and at times we live out of this self. We must admit that we commit sins!

In the gospel parables, there is one person who best typifies what it means to live out of our false self: the Prodigal Son.

---

[7]From Merton's Talks to Monks, Tape #120.

For us to be reconciled we must be willing to identify with this lost, then found, soul. Ultimately, our reconciliation comes about by the free grace of God through Jesus Christ, but for our part, we have to admit that we are in need of this reconciliation. At some time in our life, each of us has to say: "I am the prodigal Son."

The Prodigal Son

> The [prodigal] son collected all his belongings and set off to a dis-
> tant country where he squandered his inheritance on a life of
> dissipation... [there he] found himself in dire need so he hired
> himself out to one of the local citizens [Gentile] who put him on
> his farm to tend the pigs... Coming to his senses he thought... "I
> will leave this place and go to my father and say 'Father, I have
> sinned'." So he left that place and went back to his father. While
> he was still a long way off, his father saw him and moved with pity
> he ran to the boy, clasped him in his arms and kissed him ten-
> derly... "Now we must celebrate and rejoice for he was dead and has
> come to life again, he was lost and has been found." (Lk. 15:
> 11–32)

This is the story of the son who denies his true identity — he denies his
true self — and goes off into a distance country, into his false self. Wan-
dering in unreality he recalls who he truly is, his father's son, and re-
turns home to be reconciled.

The prodigal son knew he needed reconciliation just as there are
times when we know we are the prodigal son. Like him, we know what
it means to wander in a foreign land, alone and frightened, separated from
our source of life. We know what it means to be in the grips of our false
self, what it means to try "to be" of ourselves, to be our own cause, in-
dependent of God. We know what it means to commit sins.

Like the prodigal son, we must come to our senses, recognize
our state of unreality and return to our true selves. We must return to our
Father whom we have left, but who has never left us. The prodigal son
left the father; the father never left the son. He never saw him as not
being his child. To the father, his son was always his son. It was the

son who wandered and lost his identity, not the father. To the father, there never was a break in the relationship. There never was a separation between himself and his son. It was from the son's side that the un-reality occurred, so it was the son who needed the reunion, the elimination of his illusory separation.

I think it is noteworthy that in this parable the father doesn't mention any guilt because he doesn't see his son as guilty. Also he never says, "I forgive you." To have said that would have implied that the father had previously made a judgment against his son, which the father never did. The father never judged, never condemned or cut off his way-ward son.

And for us, there is even more to this story. As Christians, we know the way we prodigals are reunited with God our Father; we know the way, or how, the Father reconciles and brings us home, i.e., how the Father "restores" us to our identity which we imagine we have lost. We know and believe in Jesus Christ, our reconciliation with God.

Reconciliation

St. Paul refers to Christ as our reconciliation with God: "Jesus Christ, through Whom we have now received reconciliation" (Rom 5:11). Our reconciliation takes place when we accept our identity as God's children, or conversely, when we receive the grace to deny any imaginary separation, any split, between ourselves and God. But specifically, just how did Christ bring about the grace of our reconciliation? How did his life and death heighten that awareness of our oneness with God, increase our sense of who we are?

Our sense of identity as God's children is deadened because we imagine a distance between ourselves and God. And the result of this deadening is that it is impossible, by our powers, to be aware of our true self. We need another to lead us along the way into our identity. We need Jesus, "who leads us in our faith" (Heb 12:2 JB), or is "the pioneer...of our faith" (RSV).

Jesus also had to grow into his identity. He had to grow in the awareness of who he was: God's Son. "He grew in wisdom, age and grace" (Lk 2:52). However, once he had that awareness he held fast to it. He held fast to his identity as being one with God, whom he dared to call "Abba."

At whatever time he became fully conscious of who he was, possibly at his baptism, when he heard, "You are My beloved Son with You I am well pleased" (Mk 1:11); from that time on, he believed in his oneness with God. It is Christ's insistence on his oneness with God that is the source of that grace by which we can and must insist on our oneness with God. His steadfast claim of Sonship is the basis for the claim of our being a Child (a Son, a Daughter) of God.

128

Our reconciliation is receiving the grace to become aware of who we are, the grace of having our true identity become clear to us, the grace of accepting our union with God.

Christ won for us that grace by refusing to accept that illusion of separation and instead believing in his union with God, a union which gave him his identity as God's Son.

To express that same reality in negative terms, we can say that Christ is our reconciliation because he, unlike us, refused to engage in self-punishment, or to be self-alienated. Christ's refusal to move against himself won for us the grace by which we also can refuse to engage in self-destructiveness. For this reason, John the Baptist proclaims of him: "Behold the Lamb of God, Who takes away the *sin* of the world" (Jn 1:29).

In the context that we have been speaking, "to take away the *sin* of the world" means to dispel humankind's illusion of separation from God, thus separation from ourselves. Christ, therefore, is the source of our reconciliation, reconciliation with our true self, reconciliation with God giving us our true identity as God's sons and daughters.

We automatically assume that it was easy for Christ to arrive at, and hold fast to, his identity. But when the "Word became flesh and dwelt among us" (Jn 1:14), when the Son of God entered our human condition, he accepted that condition completely. Basic to our condition is the temptation to believe that we are split off from God, indeed that there is a split in our very being. Christ had to face what we face (he "was tempted in every way that we are" Heb 4:15) and our greatest temptation concerns our self-identity. We are always grappling with "Who are we?" Are we our true self, with God as the ground of our being, or are we our false self, that puppet of idols?

Christ's three temptations in the desert revolved around how he saw himself. The temptations concerned his identity. Was God to be the Source of his life or something else? Something else like:

Prestige — turning stones into bread (Lk 4:3);

Magic — jumping off the pinnacle of the temple (Lk 4:9); or

Power — Satan saying "I will give you all this power" (Lk 4:6).

This is our temptation also. Our false self, which believes it is separated from God, is battling our true self who is permanently united with God. This basic temptation to self-alienation comes to us through many forms, external and internal.

The external factors which serve to convince us that we are separated from God, that we are not what we should be, arise from what others tell us about ourselves. We know that children who are continually told they are bad come to believe they are. Adults feel they are failures if society tells them they are failures. We tend to see ourselves as others see us. We develop our identity, that idea of who we are, based on what others tell us about ourselves. This is especially true when these others are considered righteous and just, when it is the decent, Godly people who tell us we are good or bad. Christ, no less than we do, felt the effects of what others said about him. What were Christ's contemporaries, especially those who knew God's law, the respectable people, telling Christ about what and therefore who he was?

During his public life his reputation was that he traveled with prostitutes, had publicans in his company, and associated with Samaritans and Gentiles (always referred to as Gentile *sinners*). The Sabbath laws were God's laws handed down through Moses, and everyone knew Christ broke those laws: telling a man to carry his pallet and having his disciples pick grain on the Sabbath.

Christ himself said others referred to him as a "glutton and drunkard." Several times he was the cause of civil and religious unrest, even in the holiest of places, the synagogue and the temple. He was called a trouble-maker. Some of his relatives, to avoid condemning him outright, said, "He is out of His mind" (Mk 3:21). The religious establishment of the day said, "He is possessed by [the devil] Beelzebul" (Mk 3:22).

At the end of his life the general population joined with the respected authorities in condemning him as a sinner, as one cut off from God, and even his disciples deserted and denied they knew him. To die as a criminal, a religious heretic, a blasphemer, to be crucified, all are sure signs that such a person is separated from God. It is evident that he was not as he should be. Every Jew of the time including Jesus himself knew the word of God as recorded in sacred Scripture, "Cursed is he who is hung on a tree" (Dt 21:23). All this external evidence did point to Christ as one who was cursed, the one who was split off from life.

Besides this external evidence, however, there are even more convincing proofs of our separation from God: our sins! The most convincing evidence we have of our alienation from God comes from internal evidence, the experience of sins. Our sins are to us proof that we are cut off from God, that there is a distance between ourselves and the source of our life. I sin, therefore I am not! I am not what I should be; I am not a Child of God. I am not one who can call God "Abba."

Christ had to face this evidence also, although Christ did not sin. He accepted our condition which means he accepted our sins. Christ accepted our sins as his sins! He saw them as his own! God made Him to be sin (2 Cor 5:21). Having our sins on himself, Christ knew what it felt like to be a sinner. The prophet Isaiah foretold of the Messiah that "He would be counted among the wicked" (Is 53:12). Martin Luther, commenting on this passage, wrote:

> All the prophets did foresee that Christ should become the greatest transgressor, murderer, adulterer, thief, desecrator, blasphemer, etc., that ever was, or could be in the world... Christ was not only found among sinners, taking upon Him the flesh and blood of those which were sinners, but he would be a companion of sinners, transgressors, and plunged into all kinds of sin... He is a sinner which *hath* and *carrieth* the sins of [all]... Therefore this general sentence of Moses, "Cursed is He that hangest on a tree" (Dt 21:23), comprehendeth Christ also [albeit in his own person he was innocent] because it found Him among transgressors.[8]

Sins convince a person that he is distant from God, that he is abandoned by God. Christ shared that experience. Having all sins, of all

---

[8]Luther's commentary on St. Paul's Epistle to the Galations as reprinted in Dillenberger, *Martin Luther*, p. 135.

people, of all time as his own sins, Christ knew that experience of feeling cut off from life, even of being cursed by God. As St. Paul said, Christ became "a curse for us" (Gal 3:13). This sense of separation from God served as a temptation to Christ, a serious temptation. "My God, my God, why have You forsaken me?" (Mk 15:34).

But he overcame that temptation and held fast to his union with God, his Father. "Father, into Your hands I commend my spirit" (Lk 23:46). The overwhelming internal evidence, as well as the equally strong external evidence had to be faced by Christ. He had to confront it and deny its effect. He did both!

Despite the external evidence of suffering the shameful death reserved for the worst of criminals, i.e., being "rejected by others" (Is 53:3), despite the internal evidence of seeing all sins being on himself as his, i.e., being made "sin" (2 Cor 5:21), Christ refused to believe he was separated from or was being punished by God. Even though Scripture said he was cursed because he "hangeth on a tree," Christ refused to believe he was cursed.

From a human point of view, from our point of view, Christ was a person who was cut off from God. In the way we look at things, Christ had to be judged, had to be punished by God; after all, he did carry all of our sins on himself. If God did not judge Christ, the greatest of all "sinners," just who could he judge? If God did not condemn and punish this person, never could he condemn and punish any person. Those are the conclusions we would have to draw, had we witnessed the crucifixion. From appearances we could see only judgment, condemnation and punishment.

If we were contemporaries of Christ we would have been convinced that this man on the cross had to be under God's judgment. The more religiously correct we were, the more law-abiding, the more we would have been convinced that our perspective was correct, that God's justice was being vindicated on this man hanging on the tree.

Then something happened which proved that our perspective was not correct, that appearances are deceiving, that the human point of view is not God's point of view. Christ was raised from the dead! The fact that

Christ was raised, that therefore he was not cut off from life, not separated from God, shows us that our ideas about God are false. "Do you see now how God has shown up the foolishness of human wisdom?" (I Cor 1:20).

The resurrection shows us that our ideas, our "wisdom" about God as judge, God as condemner and punisher is foolishness, a mere fabrication of split minds. Seeing God as our judge is the hideous offspring of our inner alienation that we project onto God, making him one of the "gods," an idol, our punishing Zeus. Christ's resurrection reveals to us that when we turn God into Zeus and then believe we are condemned and cut off from our source of life, we are in a deadly illusion.

For sure we can make our illusions real, to us, and accordingly act out of our false identity. We can live out of our false self, as if we were in fact separated from God, and because of our free will God cannot change that illusion. So our sins do diminish that relationship of child to Father, but only from our side, because we believe they do. None of our illusions, however, are real to God. With him, our identity never changes.

We are always his children; he is always our Abba, our Father, who knows nothing of judgment and punishment, nothing of separation. From God's side there is never a rupture in the relationship of Father to Child. God is always Father to his sons and daughters. Christ's resurrection proved that union is eternal.

Christ, by taking our sins on himself yet still believing in his identity as God's Son, and then being raised, showed us that nothing, absolutely nothing, even our sins, can separate us from God. "If God is for us, who can be against us?" (Rom 8:31). By holding onto his identity despite all evidence to the contrary, Christ won for us the grace by which we may hold onto our identity as God's child, despite all evidence to the contrary. Our reconciliation is effected, that is, we know for sure God is our "Abba" because God is Christ's "Abba." "As proof that we are children, God sent the Spirit of His Son into our hearts, crying 'Abba, Father' " (Gal 4:6).

How could we, puny sinners that we are, be cut off from God, when Christ, the greatest of all "sinners," was not cut off? For God to be just, i.e., a "righteous judge" (I Pt 2:23), he must always be united to us because he was always united to Christ. God was always Father to Christ, the one who was, like us "born of a woman, born under the Law" (Gal 4:4), the one who like us was...born naked, and the one who...died naked.

> *Who told Christ he was naked? Who told Christ he was bad?*
> *We — humanity — did!*
>
> *Thankfully, Christ refused to believe us;*
> *He refused to believe humanity's illusions.*
>
> *Rather he believed in God's words:*
> *"You are My beloved Son, with You*
>   *I am well pleased,"[9]*
>   *and so called God, "Abba"!*
>
> *May we, in our turn, believe in God's words:*
> *"You are My beloved Son, you are My beloved Daughter,*
>   *with you I am well pleased,"*
>   *and so call God "Abba" —*
>   *right in our nakedness!*

---

[9]Mk 1:11.

Appendix

"Christ My Reconciliation"
A Meditation

Hopefully in the preceding pages we have seen that our judging is rooted in the sense of guilt and fear which is itself the result of feeling separated from God. Only a faith in who we truly are — children of God, a son or daughter of our Abba — can free us from our guilt, fear and judging syndrome.

The main focus of this book, therefore, has been on believing in our identity, in our true, Christ-centered self. As we worded it in our text, "We are our true self, but we have a false self." We must concentrate more on who we are, rather than what we have.

Some may object that although by faith we believe in our true self, what we daily experience is more often our false self. Like the prodigal son we experience our sinfulness and it is from this awareness that we feel the need of Christ to reconcile us to God. For us then to accept the fact of our reconciliation, it is not sufficient to remain on the level of reason; we have to experience it.

Important as theological explanations may be, in themselves they aren't going to convince us that we are loved, that we are united to God. We have to move from the head to the heart to feel what the prodigal son felt when he was welcomed home by his father.

For this reason I have added this appendix, a meditation on Christ as our reconciliation. We will use as our starting point St. Paul's statement "He [God] made Him [Christ] to be sin" (2 Cor 5:21). It is important to keep in mind, however, that "sin" here is what we have called "sins." Christ became those sins, those destructive thoughts, words and deeds which we commit and which give rise to further guilt.

God the Father brings us back through Christ assuming our sins, appropriating our guilt. Christ became the prodigal son with us so we might become the true "son" or daughter with him, the One brought back, the One welcomed home, the One reconciled.

We should consider ourselves as "dead men brought back to life" (Rom 6:13 JB). For with Christ we "have been brought back to true life" (Col 3:1 JB).

Christ, by becoming "sin" (*sins* in this meditation), is how and the way our false self, that prodigal part of ourselves, which we accept but God doesn't, is brought back home to the Father. Christ is the way we are reunited to the Father who has always been our home, and from whom we have never been really separated. Let us conclude with a meditation on this paradox. Since a meditation is personal, this has been written in the first person, "I." My reconciliation is something only I can experience.

Christcame Became Sin

My reconciliation with God hinges on the mystery of Christ becoming sin, becoming sin even to the degree that Paul refers to Him as "the cursed one": "Christ by becoming a curse for us" (Gal 3:13 RSV).

Christ so identified himself with me, as sinner, that he became the one who is cursed.

Christ, the innocent one, took on himself my lack of innocence, took on himself my guilt, so I could, in him, be innocent, in him be guiltless.

Christ has taken my sin and given me his righteousness, taken my guilt and given me his innocence.

Christ, who did not sin, willed to be counted among sinners. He accepted my lot. He stepped into my position. Although innocent in himself, Christ accepted the curse of *my* guilt.

Reconciliation involves an exchange, with Christ being at the center. He is the focus who bears my sins, so that God's righteousness may be mine.

"He [God] made Him [Christ] to be sin…so that in Christ we might become the righteousness of God" (2 Cor 5:21 RSV).

In Divine reconciliation one thing is, so that another may be.

The Innocent One — Christ — becomes the guilty one, so that the guilty one — I — become the innocent one: "Christ…giving Himself up in our place" (Eph 5:1 JB).

My sin and death — the slavery of self-punishment — is exchanged for Christ's grace and life — the freedom of salvation. "You have been freed from the slavery of sin" (Rom 6:18 JB). It is a life-giving exchange where my trespasses are not counted against me.

"In Christ God was reconciling the world to Himself, not counting their trespasses against them" (2 Cor 5:19 RSV).

I am reconciled solely because my trespasses are counted not against me, but against Christ. My trespasses are laid on Christ and not on me.

I am saved for no other reason.

The Love of Christic

The fact that my sins are laid on Christ and his righteousness on me is not as easy for me as it might first appear, as if I had nothing to do in this exchange. I do have something to do! To avail myself of God's reconciliation I must fulfill a condition, a difficult — a crucifying — condition!

In order for Christ to take upon himself all that is mine, I must take upon myself all that is mine. For Christ to be one with me, I must be one with me. That's difficult!

In order for me to exchange with Christ, I must accept and love myself as Christ accepts and loves me. To accept and love myself as Christ accepts and loves me — that's crucifying! It implies: I must admit what I am, accept myself as I am, and love who I am.

When Christ joined himself to me he took upon himself all that I do not want to admit and accept about myself. He became me. So now, the only way I can be one with Christ is to take upon myself all that I do not want to admit and accept about myself — and become me.

To be united with Christ, then, I must become a creature. I must become flesh and blood — contingent! I must become a finite being with all the insecurities, weaknesses and resulting fears that state implies.

For love of me, "the Word became flesh and made his dwelling among us" (Jn 1:14). So now, for love of me, *I* must become flesh and dwell among us. That is exactly what I think I should not be, and who I do not want to be — a human being.

Christ's acceptance and love of me demands I accept and love my own humanity. Accepting and loving my humanity is humiliating. It strips me of my idealized self-image: that illusion I have created to sustain and support myself; that ideal image; that phantom of power I have manufactured for my support and protection; that picture of perfection I have painted for my sense of security; that false self; that self I think I should be.

That's what I am stripped of when I condescend to become "flesh and dwell among us." That's a shameful stripping! It leaves me naked, with no covering, embarrassingly exposed. It leaves me a poor person, unpretentiously honest, totally defenseless. It leaves me a human being!

I must admit: I do not accept that stripping. I do not accept my humanity. I do not accept what Christ accepted — my poverty.

I refuse to be a "poor person." I refuse to be myself. I refuse to be so humiliated. I refuse to be what I think I "should not be." Instead, I rebel at the weakness of my condition. I try to escape my vulnerable state. And it is right there — in my attempt to escape — that evil lies. Evil lies coiled around my attempt to escape my kind, to escape what I am — a limited being, destined to die!

Eat the fruit and "you shall be like gods" (Gn 3:5). "To be like the gods!" That's my goal! Power! That's my aim! I want to rise above my humanity, with its imperfections and limitations, its dark spots and defects. To rise above my creatureliness, my mortality, that's what I want — "to die not!" Immortality!

When God became man, became the "Son of Man," He became "obedient to death, even death on a cross" (Phil 2:8). That is, he accepted, loved and held onto my condition; he made my state, a state bounded by death — his own. He obeyed human life, and human death.

"Learn of me," he said, "for I am meek and humble of heart" (Mt 11:29). But I refuse to learn of Christ and his humility, refuse to become obedient, refuse to die.

Humbly obey my condition? Hold onto my state? Accept and love who I am, what I am? Die?

No! Absolutely not! I reject it all. I deny it. I rebel against it. I want to be "like the gods" — strong, right, perfect — all those things I think

I should be. I do not want to be a human being — weak, wrong, imperfect — all those things I think I should not be. It is as simple as that.

I reject the truth of my state, which means, I live falsely; which means, I lie; which means, I move against myself. In other words — I sin! Unhesitatingly, I must admit — "I sin!" Unceasingly, I must admit — "I sin!" This admission means I spiritually hit bottom.

In Christian language, it is crucifying. In Jewish language, it is being the prodigal son, tending swine for the Gentiles. Pigs and Gentiles! That's hitting bottom! No Jew could hit bottom with a greater thud.

Christ became sin. He hit bottom to find me. I have to admit, that is the only place he can find me. No salvation is possible without this uncomfortable fact — I can be found only on the bottom.

No reconciliation is possible without this thud.

Faith in Jesus Christ

But certainly it is not merely being a prodigal, not merely knowing my sin, not merely going thud which effects reconciliation. Of itself, all that brings is more guilt — more sin! Unresolved guilt produces sin! In fact, I sin because I am trying to escape from, or compensate for, a sense of guilt and shame. Sin is a compensatory device.

The greater my sense of guilt or shame (for being inferior to "the gods"), the greater will be my compulsion to compensate.

There is a sense of pain underneath each sin. There is a sense of guilt that is prior to each offense. And if this wound is not brought to consciousness and to the healing of God's reconciliation, it will continually influence me.

The more guilt, the more shame I have hidden deep within me, the more I will be driven to sin. In a futile attempt to escape my pain, I will move against myself and consequently others. This move is sin!

When my guilt and shame for being a human being becomes too intense, I will be tempted to step out of my condition. This step is sin! This is why God's reconciliation does not settle in shame. I am not called to wallow in guilt. Guilt and shame are not the last word — Faith is! Faith defuses guilt! Faith repudiates shame! Faith in Christ who stood in my stead — that faith is the last word.

For, once I have faith in Christ's identification with me, to the degree of even becoming sin, I can then claim Christ as my own. Since Christ claimed me as his own, I can claim him as my own. Since Christ became the sinner, I became the righteous one. Since Christ took my guilt and shame, I am freed of guilt and shame, freed of sin — justified — once I believe!

My reconciliation comes about through faith. My salvation takes place once I believe that Christ has joined himself to me, in my sin, thereby ensuring the Father's love for me, in my sin.

My sins are mine — nobody else's! Nobody else's except — Jesus Christ's! My sin is Christ's sin — now. Christ's righteousness is my righteousness — now.

Grace makes this so. Faith makes this so. Through faith I become one with Christ and he with me, so that when the Father looks upon me he sees Christ. That is, if I have faith in Jesus Christ and his oneness with me, if I believe that "I live, no longer I, but Christ lives in me" (Gal 2:20), believe that "in Christ, God has chosen us before the world was made" (Eph 1:4); believe that "God has blessed us in Christ with every spiritual blessing" (Eph 1:3 RSV). If I believe!

Faith is the last word! It's the means, the only means to escape the prodigal's thud of guilt, sin, and finally, self-destruction.

My faith in "Him whom God has sent" is the only way I can be reconciled.

Faith of Jesus Christ

But even "my" faith is not all *my* doing. In fact, "my" faith is really not mine at all. "My" faith includes, and actually is, the faith of Jesus. Reconciliation takes place when I have both: faith *in* Jesus and the faith *of* Jesus. It's the same faith, but I couldn't have it unless Christ had it first, showing and giving me the way.

Paul reminds us of this faith of Jesus and how he leads us in our faith. "Let us not lose sight of Jesus, who is the pioneer of our faith, who leads us in our faith" (Heb 12:2), "who offered up prayers and entreaty, with cries, to the one who had the power to save Him from death" (Heb 5:7).

Yes, let us not lose sight of the faith *of* Jesus "who when he was tortured put His trust [his faith] in the righteous judge" (1 Pt 2:23 JB).

My faith is believing in Christ, who himself believed in the Father's saving love. Christ, laden with my sins as he was, still believed in the Father's love for him. Now his faith becomes my faith. Christ and I both have the same faith in the same Father, because we both have the same sin.

Christ assumed my sin and "put His faith in the righteous judge" so I, even in my sin, can have that same faith. My faith is believing with the faith of Jesus in the Father, "the one who had the power to save him [thus, *me*] from death."

The fact that Jesus, who wrapped himself in sin, indeed became the sinner of all time, still believed in the Father and so was raised, gives me the surety I will be raised. I too will be made righteous and sanctified. For I know God made Christ "our righteousness and our sanctification" (I Cor 1:30 JB). I know that "He who raised up the Lord Jesus will raise me up along with Jesus" (2 Cor 4:14), and I know that if Christ the sinner, the one "made to be sin," was raised and sanctified, I will be too.

For "the Father has brought us to life with Christ" (Col 2:13)...that is, if I believe as Christ did, if I allow Christ's faith and trust to become mine.

Faith *in* Jesus Christ is the last word. The faith *of* Jesus Christ is the last word. To believe *in* Jesus Christ is to believe *with* Jesus Christ. My faith *is* Christ's faith.

The Christian Paradox

My faith, my reconciliation, however, is only a part of a much larger paradox — Christianity itself. Christianity is the paradox of all time: that tragic comedy where Christians are always lost, yet always found; always dead, yet always alive; always crucified, yet always risen; always sinner, yet always justified.

I am a sinner! Always!

"All have sinned and are deprived of the glory of God" (Rom 3:23). "They are all under the domination of sin...there is no one just, not one" (Rom 3:9, 10). Yet I am justified! Always!

"God justifies everyone who believes in Jesus" (Rom 3:26 JB), and it's the same justification "that comes through faith to everyone who believes in Jesus" (Rom 3:22 JB); "Through Christ justification from all sins...is offered to every believer" (Acts 13:38 JB); "There is no condemnation for those who are in Christ" (Rom 8:1).

Sinner, yet justified? Always? At the same time? That's illogical, if not an outright contradiction. Always a prodigal, yet always reconciled? It doesn't make any sense.

Am I surprised at that? Did Christ, has Christianity, ever made sense?

Since when is faith logical? It is totally illogical to believe that to be saved by God's righteousness, I must become unrighteous. To be saved by God's grace, I must become graceless. To be saved from sin, I must become sin.

It is totally illogical to believe that only the sinner is saved, the lost found, the dead alive, only the prodigal reconciled. It is totally illogical

to believe that for me to be saved from my sin I must be joined to Christ as sinner — mine actual, his assumed.

It is totally illogical, on both my part and Christ's. Totally illogical, but true! The Christian paradox: if I am to be one with Christ in his resurrection, I must be willing to be one with Christ in "his" sin — my sin that he took upon himself — as "his."

Or, as Paul says, only "if we have been united with Him in a death like His, we will certainly be united with Him in a resurrection like His" (Rom 6:5 RSV).

Resurrection implies that I am willing to see myself as the prodigal; I must become the sinner, so that I have nothing, absolutely nothing, to claim before God. I have nothing — except the righteousness of Christ, which is everything. Nothing yet everything; everything *through* nothing. Reconciliation through sin. Salvation through guilt. Freedom through shame.

The only way out is *through*. To be rid of it, I must claim it. Illogical? Indeed it is! It is as illogical as saying "All have sinned" (Rom 3:23), yet "those who have been born of God do not sin" (I Jn 3:9 RSV).

The Christian paradox.

The Last Temptation

But is faith before such a paradox possible? To be reconciled, I must become guilty? To be saved, I must become sin? That is just too extreme to be believed.

Can God's love for me be that strong? Can God's faithfulness to me be that enduring? It's absurd — a contradiction — a scandal! The last temptation! My last temptation!

"Though your sins be like scarlet, they shall be white as snow" (Is 1:18 RSV). *Unbelievable!* "Where sin abounded, grace did more abound" (Rom 5:20 Douay). *Impossible!*

Everyone's last temptation! Christ's last temptation! Christ who was himself "tempted in every way we are" (Heb 4:15 JB); Christ who said, "blessed is the one who takes no offense at me [he who is not scandalized in me]" (Lk 7:23); who then prayed, "my God, my God, why have you forsaken me?" (Mk 15:34) — that Christ is a scandal.

Christianity is a scandal. The scandalous paradox, where God made Christ to be sin. The very one who did not sin "was made to be sin" so that I, the one who does sin, am reconciled with God.

I am to be reconciled with God? I — so loved? So forgiven?

God "having forgiven us all our trespasses" (Col 2:13), "your sins I will remember no more" (Is 43:25). "I will never call their sins to mind" (Heb 10:17).

I can't believe it. "My God, my God, why have you forsaken me?" (Mk 15:34). Yet Christ, living within me, he can believe it. "Father, into your hands I commend my Spirit" (Lk 23:46).

150

Because Christ trusted as no one has ever trusted; he trusted that "the One who made the promise is faithful" (Heb 10:23). Christ, "the one who leads us in our faith," he can believe it again — in me.

"Let us not lose sight of Jesus." Yes, for only *in* Jesus is my salvation possible; only *in* Jesus is my reconciliation with God believable.

Thanks Be To God

Reconciliation rests on the fact that "God made Him to be sin" — and not on the fact that I do not sin! *Thanks be to god.*

I am saved, not because I am strong, perfect, and right (the elder son), but because God made Christ to be weak, imperfect, and wrong — the prodigal son. *Thanks be to God.*

Salvation is not given to me because of my good works, or because of my virtue. *Thanks be to God.*

I am saved by grace, and faith in Jesus Christ — and nothing else! "For by grace you have been saved through faith, and this is not your own doing" (Eph 2:8 RSV). "This is not your own doing." *Thanks be to God.*

God's reconciliation does not rest on what we humans do, as if human activity could merit Divine reconciliation, as if what I do could merit the Father's love.

I merit my reconciliation? Does the clay merit the potter, the portrait the artist? Does the son merit the father, the sinner, reconciliation? That's nonsense, utter nonsense! *Thanks be to God.*

"Always be thankful" (Col 3:15 JB). Then Paul exclaims, "thanks be to God who gives us the victory through our Lord Jesus Christ" (1 Cor 15:57 RSV). "Gives us the victory." Reconciliation is God's gift — a gift! Not merited!

"It is by grace you have been saved, through faith, and this is not your own doing but a *gift* from God" (Eph 2:8 RSV). "It's God's free gift to us in His beloved" (Eph 1:6), and as God's beloved, "Jesus Christ will cause everyone to reign in life who receives this free gift, which he does not deserve" (Rom 5:17 JB).

So now, all the prodigals, myself, Paul, everyone who receives "this free gift which he does not deserve," can exclaim — *Thanks be to God.*

Thanks be to God through our Lord Jesus Christ. For he is the one who is not ashamed of our humanity, who, unlike us, is not the least bit ashamed of our nakedness.